Hidden Triumph
in
Ethiopia

Hidden Triumph
in
Ethiopia

KAY BASCOM

William Carey Library
PASADENA · CALIFORNIA

Hidden Triumph
in
Ethiopia

Published by:

William Carey Library
P.O. Box 40129
Pasadena, CA 91114 USA
Phone: 626.798.0819 • Email: publishing@wclbooks.com

Library of Congress Cataloging–in–Publication Data

Bascom, Kaythryn, 1931-
    Hidden Triumph in Ethiopia / Kathryn Bascom
        p. cm.
    ISBN 0-87808-606-4 (alk. paper)
    1. Negussie Kumbi, d. 1993. 2. Christian Biography —Ethiopia. 3. Communism and Christianity—Ethiopia. I. Title

    BR1725.N42 B37 2001
    281'.75'092—dc21
    [B]
                                                                2001026930

Cover Design: Mark Sequeira
Maps: Johnathan Bascom
Book Design & Layout : D.M. Battermann, R&D Design Services

Printed in the United States of America

Table of Contents

164850

ABBREVIATIONS

BBC — British Broadcasting Company

CIA — Central Intelligence Bureau (of the USA)

EAL — Ethiopian Air Lines

ELF — Eritrean Liberation Front

EPLF — Eritrean Peoples Liberation Front

EPRDF— Ethiopian People's Revolutionary Democratic Front (*Yehadig*)

GBI — Grace Bible Institute

HQ — short for "Headquarters"

IEC — International Evangelical Church

KHC — Kale Heywet Church

KHDP— Kale Heywet Development Program

MAF — Missionary Aviation Fellowship

OAU — Organization of African Unity

PMAC— Provisional Military Administrative Council *(Derg)*

RAF — Royal Air Force - British

RVOG — Radio Voice of the Gospel (Lutheran station, Addis Ababa)

SIM — Sudan Interior Mission previously, changed to Society for International Ministries

TPLF — Tigray People's Liberation Front

TTI — Teachers Training Institute

Figure 1. Area of the Great Rift, from Israel through Ethiopia (Pre-1991).

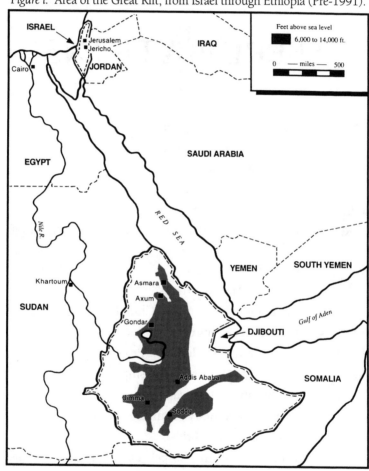

Source: Adapted from *"The Jews of Ethiopia"*, 1986.

Figure 2. Map of Ethiopia, major locations mentioned in the text.

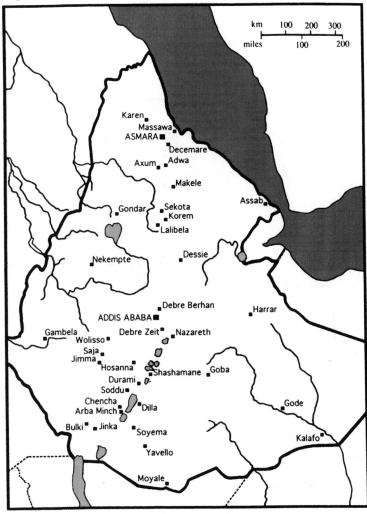

Figure 3. Traditional regional boundaries of Ethiopian provinces.

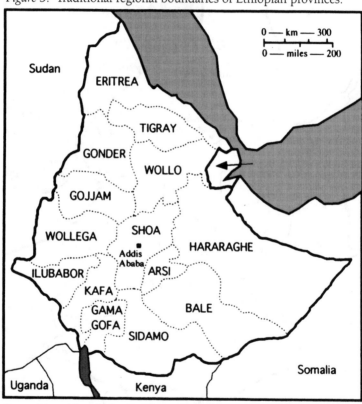

Source: Adapted from Parker, B., *Ethiopia: Breaking New Ground,* Oxfam, 1995.

ACKNOWLEDGMENTS

This manuscript has come about by metamorphosis. It began with an invitation from John Cumbers to help him with a book he was writing about the Ethiopian church during the Marxist Revolution, during which time he was our mission's East African Field Director. That book was published in 1995 under the title, "Count It All Joy." As I helped check Mr. Cumbers' interviews and as I added new ones, talking with over 150 people, the composite story of the church in this period challenged me deeply. I became convinced it begged to be heard by people unfamiliar with Ethiopia. But how to catch the interest of such readers was a problem.

Advisors suggested I simplify the task by writing it as historical fiction, an approach popular with readers today. Some wonderful books have been written in this mode about the Ethiopian saga. My calling, however, was to report facts, not devise fiction — even if true to the spirit of the facts — in order to authenticate another chapter of God's "acts of the apostles" in this generation.

The advice I finally did take, however, was to select one person's story and build a shorter book around that life. I chose Negussie Kumbi's life as a uniquely fitted vehicle for telling the Ethiopian story.

I tried to find the drama already imbedded in the story and let it make its own statement. I've limited dialogue to conversations actually reported to me, and when I've suggested thoughts, they are obvious ones framed in elemental forms.

Hundreds of Ethiopians and expatriates graciously gave their time to doing the interviews out of which the book emerged — all the people who appear in the story, and others regretfully unmentioned, some of whose lives were not directly linked with Negussie's, but whose information corroborated the facts or helped me realize that Negussie was representative of many Ethiopian Christians. Only one name is given for most of those who are identified in the story, as a slight precaution. Travelers from abroad such as Yu Kwong and Lily Hsueh, Chris Ott Weber, and Soula Isch made fortuitous visits to Ethiopia while I was collecting information there and furnished additional pieces of Negussie's story. To all those who spent hours answering questions and volunteering significant information, I am deeply grateful.

My greatest challenge was to piece together all the happenings and characters as I ferreted out the story. Missionaries Murray, Bea, and John Coleman and Ted Veer related much from Negussie's early life. Negussie's wife Fantaye Mogus (with Haregwein translating), Ato Tekle Wolde Giorgos, Mulugeta Haile, Sahle Tilahun, Mina Moen, Paul and Lila Balisky, Bruce and Betty Adams, and others provided personal details from his adult life and glimpses of shared experiences. Those of us who have been involved in some way with this project have become kind of a relay team to make the story known. Negussie ran the first lap; those whose lives intersected his have fleshed out the story as they ran intermediate laps; and I've tried to carry the baton across the finish line.

We have had coaches and trainers as well — John Cumbers and Harold Fuller encouraging and supervising this effort; Johnathan Bascom smoothing out computer intricacies; Harold Fuller and Tim Bascom editing sections of the manuscript; Paul and Barbara Entz, Ron Frazee, Thelma Kephart, Brad Lapsley, Bikat Sahle and Julie Norbury giving editorial advice. In the stands, others like Hans Hagen, Dieter Schmoll, Art Volkmann, Carol Plueddemann, and Sandi Dick have cheered us on. I am deeply grateful to Rick Kress, Director of William Carey Library, for his labors to bring this Ethiopian testimony to publication. Many have prayed about the book. I am especially aware of an Intermission Prayer band in Ethiopia; and in Kansas, Leroy and Blanche Davis, Margaret Burton, Dot Taylor, and prayer groups in our home church. Most patient and supportive in the long process has been my husband, Charles, who has shared the deep love for the people of Ethiopia that God gave us together.

When J. B. Phillips translated the New Testament into modern English, he said he felt like an electrician wiring an old house with the mains left on. As I spent hour after hour listening to the experiences of Ethiopian Christians, I felt as if I was touching God's household of faith "with the mains left on." My hope is that the current I encountered may be transferred to readers. Entering into this modern chapter of Acts, may we see the Light of the world shining therein, and in our own dark corners be bearers of His current.

Kay Bascom

AUTHOR'S
INTRODUCTION

Hidden Triumph in Ethiopia is the story of Negussie Kumbi, (pronounced Ne güs´ se Küm´ bi) an unlikely hero with a body twisted by childhood disease, but it is Ethiopia's story too. Negussie's adulthood paralleled the Revolution, the period of the communications blackout in Ethiopia.

His life serves as a metaphor for the Christians of Ethiopia — or any other community in vital union with Christ: broken of body yet straight of soul; poor yet rich; captive yet free; prepared for death, yet alive. From the book of Acts, we see that God wants His people's stories passed on, learned from, and enjoyed throughout the world, and in each generation.

Long before hearing of Negussie, my husband and I lost our hearts to Ethiopia. It happened in 1964, when we first went to Africa. Although I had grown up attending church and thought Jesus to have been a significant historical character, I did not come to know Him as a living person until college years. I began to pore over the Gospel of John, studying it as determinedly as my college courses, and then moved on to Acts. There I was exposed to the kind of believers whom I longed to find on earth now. Where do you find such a community, I wondered, among people in the 100th-some generation of Christianity?

God answered my longing in a strange way. I met a medical student, Charles Bascom, who also had just come alive to the Lord Jesus and we soon married.

Eventually Charles was invited to do short term medical service in Ethiopia. We embarked, thinking ourselves "haves" going to "have nots." We ended up working among one of the southern tribes of Ethiopia. I was assigned to teach English in the mission school across the dusty road from the hospital where Charles worked, the only one in the midst of a million people whose grass huts dotted the mountains and valleys of beautiful Wallamo (now called Wolaitta).

One day government officials came to investigate why our students – members of a barely literate southern "slave" tribe — seemed more interested in literacy than young people in the "establishment" tribes up north. Our students answered their question as if it should be no mystery. "Why? Well, since we've discovered that God sent humanity a message, we want to be able to read it for ourselves!" How reasonable, I thought, realizing how nearly lost this kind of reasonableness now is, in the West. Repeatedly, questions of first-generation Christians shook up the foreigners. When missionaries first reached this animistic area in 1927, the Ethiopians asked them, "Why did it take Christians nearly 2000 years to get to us?"

In such experiences, Charles and I were finding ourselves face to face with first generation believers "in their first love" for the Lord Jesus Christ. They knew the same Savior I knew, only better than I did, I realized. This was raw Christianity! By raw I don't mean uncivilized — they were more genteel than we were — I mean "fresh," not boiled for 2000 years. We were magnetized by the Lord these people knew, so we kept our compass tuned to Ethiopia over the next thirty years, whether in or out of the country.

In the mid 1960s, we went to our first Ethiopian baptism. With hundreds of believers dressed in Ethiopia's white cotton clothing gathered at the river, the scene appeared like one out of the first century. We met Wandaro there, whose family hung him over a fire when he was among the first ten men in the tribe to profess Christ. He was always smiling in spite of teeth kicked out in prison during the Italian occupation (1937-1941). He'd led his mountain community to Christ, including a chieftain who had owned slaves. We met passionate barefoot evangelists, reminiscent of the Apostle Paul, who had risked going to fierce tribes and endured beatings and imprisonment. We bowed our heads with a dear old farmer who stood beside his donkey and took off his hat to pray after unloading a loving gift for us — a sack of potatoes from his crop.

The amazing thing about such elemental, "early" Christians is that persecution only makes them more faithful and strong. In the mid 1970s a Marxist Revolution swept through Ethiopia, putting Christians at risk just as Chinese and Romanian Christians had been threatened in the 1950s. As the Red Terror heightened, we saw Christians forced underground. Most of them stood steady and deepened. Their suffering pruned and purified them. Then they multiplied, as persecution fanned the fire of their faith.

In the mid 1980s, from back in the States we watched the East African nightmare of famine, displacement, and war. Charles was able to return and do relief work several summers, but he had to keep a distance from believers to keep from endangering them.

The government had nailed shut all the churches of our beloved Wolaitta, had repressed Christians and imprisoned many. With "the Cultural Revolution" came more suffering: "villagization" and "resettlement" displaced hundreds of thousands who were already destitute through the wars and famines that were thundering over the whole Horn of Africa.

At last in 1991, the Mengistu government collapsed. Quiet reports over the years from those few expatriates who had been able to stay in Ethiopia had been reassuring. Despite seventeen years of Marxism and its chaotic effect on many, Christians had been brought to a deep maturity and dependence upon God. We were drawn back and on our return, found the underground church bursting into the open with a passionate commitment to seize the day. Believers traveled to the unreached tribes of their land, determined to communicate God's message and treasuring the freedom to do so.

With the fall of the Marxist government, finally the Revolution years' stories could come out into the open. I first heard Negussie's story from John Coleman, a fellow student in an Amharic language refresher course in 1994. This Ethiopian's life gripped and challenged me, even though I had never met him. I knew others like him, and his story seemed to speak for them all. Throughout those "silenced" years, I had longed to give voice to the story of the Ethiopian church. I felt I had a debt to pay — a debt to Ethiopian believers for demonstrating the sufficiency of Christ to us; a debt to American believers who sent us to Ethiopia; and a debt to our Lord for having so creatively answered my hungering prayer.

All this was incubating in my mind as I worked with John Cumbers, former East African SIM director, on his book about the church during the Revolution, "Count It All Joy." In another document, I tried to get the historical progression and personal testimonies of hundreds of people woven together for Western readers. It grew longer and longer. "Stop!" I was advised. "There's too much to absorb. For starters, just tell one man's story." And so I chose Negussie's.

FLASH F■RWARD

Negussie lay in a heap where the Marxist cadres dumped him. Was he unconscious or dead? They didn't care. They laughed at his name, which meant "my king." Somebody's *Negus,* was he? They'd teach him!

Negussie's blood had dripped a trail from the torture room, and now oozed slowly from his lacerated body, dampening the prison floor. Unaware even of where he was, he lay there, beyond thought or movement, lying in the shadow of his own death.

What came to his clouded mind as consciousness flickered into his battered head? Was it just the simple awareness of blood blinding his eyes, or the pulsing pain returning to the torn soles of his feet? His legs were swollen to twice their size. He could hardly believe they were so large — like wet logs.

How could they have done this to him, he wondered. How could his own people have treated him like this? All because he gave away some New Testaments? Because he had refused to say a few words denying God? How, in a country where "God be praised" traditionally preceded every greeting, could this madness be happening...this "Red Terror"?

Was amazement his thought, amazement that he was still alive? Was it fear of another volley of the unrelenting blows that had exhausted even his torturers? Or might it have been a stab of identification with thousands of other prisoners who had undergone this kind of torture...or perhaps a visceral sense of entering into his Savior's suffering?

He could not stand. They had destroyed the bottoms of his feet. So he lay there and reviewed his life, left with nothing else to consider but himself and God.

A ROYAL
DESTINY?

In a small village of central Ethiopia in around 1950, a new-born child opened his eyes on the world. His cries rang out in the mud hut of a peasant family who subsisted on what they could grow on their small acreage beside a nearby stream. Life was elemental. As the morning mists arose from the cool valleys, the baby could smell his mother's coffee roasting over a three-stone fire base on the dirt floor of their circular hut. By day he could hear her grinding grain outside their door. By night, he could hear the peaceful breathing of cattle that his father barricaded within, safe from hyenas.

The couple named their son "Negussie" (pronounced Ne güs´ se Küm´ bi). The name's root meant "king," and its ending meant "my." In Ethiopia, nearly every child's name has a meaning. Negussie was not an unusual name, for the concept of royalty was ingrained in the country's culture. It reached back almost three thousand years to the national epic. A royal son had been born to Israel's King Solomon and Ethiopia's Queen of Sheba, the epic said. Wasn't Sheba's visit to Solomon's court recorded in the Holy Scriptures themselves, in I Kings, chapter 10?

Negussie's parents had seen Haile Selassie take Ethiopia back from Italian occupation just a decade before their baby's birth. The child's grandparents had seen Haile Selassie's predecessor,

Menelik, unify the nation the generation before. Over the vast tangled mountains and dry savannas, provincial dukes had fought for centuries for control over Ethiopia, some of them from the Amhara tribe of the central highlands, others from various outer regions. In the 1920s, the duke named *Ras Tafari* — of the Amhara ethnic group — had risen above all the others to claim supremacy. He'd used every opportunity to buttress his political power with historical credentials. He'd reached back to the Queen of Sheba's child from Solomon to claim her line by appropriating for himself the Jewish title, "Lion of Judah." In addition he'd chosen the name *Haile Selassie* ("power from the Trinity") for himself, to emphasize a Christian mandate as well.

Few rural Ethiopians were literate, but they knew their oral histories and ancestry. Around their fires at night, the stories were rehearsed. Each tribal group had its unique heritage, and rarely did tribes encourage intermarriage. Baby Negussie's mother was of the Amhara tribe, and his father, *Ato* Kumbi (ie., Mr. Kumbi), was of the Oromo tribe, not an easy alliance. According to the common Oromo custom, Kumbi kept one wife managing a compound at one of his acreages, and another wife elsewhere. His family identified loosely as Ethiopian Orthodox Christians but, along with many, lived in fear of the ancient spirits of animism. It must have deeply grieved and even frightened the family when their child's development seemed stunted, his back bent and his body compacted. Eventually Negussie was placed at Ato Kumbi's property near the small town of Wolisso, instead of living with his birth mother. Although there was a mission clinic within minutes of Negussie's home, the fear of vengeful spirits kept the family from seeking medical help.

Outside their grass-roofed hut, head-high *inset* plants (false banana) circled the home. Their broad leaves provided an African variety of disposable plates, and foods made from its root kept people alive in hard times. A few corn stalks dotted the small acreage beyond the well-swept circle where the compound's women did their daily work. Negussie's older stepmother was not fond of the child with a deformed spine who sat hunched over in the shadows of their round one-room home. Perhaps that was why, when it was not raining, Negussie liked to perch crookedly on a three-legged stool in a spot of sunshine at the gate of the compound fence. Sometimes the nurse from the Obi clinic next door passed by and would see the boy sitting there, smiling brightly.

One day she asked him, "Whose child are you?"

"I'm God's child," was his unexpected, happy response.

Stopping to visit a bit, the nurse could observe that the tiny boy showed signs of TB of the spine. She told the family that he could be helped if he got to the TB treatment center in the capital, a hundred miles away. When Negussie was about four, his parents finally did let her take him to that hospital. A few months later, the child returned from Addis Ababa with his TB arrested. At least his legs would grow, even if his torso could not develop normally.

Because the mission offered elementary schooling right next to Negussie's home, he was able to begin an education, an opportunity that the majority of Ethiopian children did not enjoy. Under the green, yellow, and red striped Ethiopian flag that waved in the schoolyard, classes were held in a simple tin-roofed building constructed from eucalyptus poles. Inside, the classrooms were simple: rough desks and benches, pencils and tablets, and a blackboard and chalk for the teacher. Among other eager students, Negussie learned to read, write, and do arithmetic. His horizons widened.

Negussie had grown up as nearly a "town kid," for Wolisso was only five kilometers from his home. He was regularly drawn by the scent of red peppers and onions to the open markets where a myriad of products were set out for display on the ground: piles of eggs and potatoes, stacks of tea cups and rat-traps, assorted soap bars and tin basins, halters and horseshoes. All this in the midst of a colorful jumble of people making their way between bleating sheep, clucking chickens, and hordes of flies buzzing around the butchers' stalls. He dodged lorries on the tarmac road through Wolisso, stood enthralled before the shelves of shops that lined the road, heard radio music pouring out of the noisy bars, and admired the muscles of men who lifted heavy sacks of grain onto the backs of donkeys.   From restaurants, he could smell the enticing aroma of hot peppery sauces eaten with flatbread, Ethiopia's best-known national dish, *injera b' wut.* He stared at faces looking out the windows of overloaded buses, strangers on their way to the wider world. He wondered about that world, even though he could boast having been to the capital once himself, for his TB treatment.

In school, the boy began to learn about clocks, measurements, and directions. On the colorful map of Ethiopia painted on the school's outside wall, he could now locate Wolisso in the center of his country. His town was just southwest of the capital on the Jimma Road, one of Ethiopia's five or so main roads that undulated over the mountains from the hub, like the limp legs of a drowned spider. He could see the string of lakes made by "the Great Rift" which cut southward from Israel through Ethiopia and on to Mozambique. But for him, leaving this little town and its marketplace seemed an unlikely possibility. He didn't even know yet what difference it made whether one was classed from the "north" or the "south" — that is, whether from Orthodox Christian Amhara territory, or from the southern tribes which were more likely to be animistic or Muslim. He didn't know that the region of Eritrea in the north was not happy to be part of the larger nation.

Among his neighborhood classmates who were mostly Oromo, Negussie stood out, not so much because of his bent spine, but due to his untroubled spirit and sunny temperament. Very early he had been tried by illness and rejection, and yet had come forth shining like gold. Negussie had an uncanny wisdom about him. "I'm God's child," he would say with happy certainty.

COLOR-BLIND
BONDING

When Negussie was eleven or twelve, a foreign family moved into the mission property next door. The lad watched the foreigners pile out of a vehicle and start settling their belongings into one of the mission's square, whitewashed, mud-and-wattle houses. It had a tin roof and a side chimney, just like the one next door where the clinic nurse and schoolteacher lived. Negussie's stepbrother and stepsister from the other wife had gone away for schooling, making him the solitary child in the home. Shyly, the hunched boy with the wide smile got acquainted with the three children — a girl about ten, a boy around six, and a toddler son. The Colemans turned out to be from far-off Canada and had lived in Addis previously. Their children began to bond with the winsome Negussie, especially the older boy, John.

National children loved to touch John's blond head and giggle as they felt the light, flimsy hair of *Yohannis,* as they called him. He didn't mind, for he was an outgoing boy with a naive and accepting nature. He had a way of turning his head around slowly as if searching for clues. The tendency was later traced to the congenital absence of a stapes bone in his right ear, which made him struggle to know from which direction sounds were coming.

Bea and Murray Coleman gathered neighborhood children for a couple weeks of daily Bible curriculum during the rainy season school recess. Negussie was already tender to God, and he was among those who indicated a commitment of their lives to the Lord Jesus Christ during that time.

Bea sought to shepherd him spiritually, in practical ways. For instance, she realized from the amount of time he spent at their home, that he must be doing very little to help at home. On chatting about it one day, he admitted he didn't help much. Since he wanted to see his parents come alive to a personal relationship with God, Bea encouraged him to demonstrate the change Christ was making in his life by helping with practical chores, carrying water or wood or helping with cattle herding whenever he could, to show them his love and respect.

The Coleman kids didn't have a lot of toys, but they shared their big red wagon and tree swing with the neighborhood children. They played "store" in the spreading branches of a sycamore outside the nurse's house, selling wares from their perches — seeds or rocks or leaves, or whatever they could think of to trade. Sounding much like the plethora of birds twittering around them, the children chattered together in a mixture of three languages: Oromo, Amharic, and English.

Negussie carried the little ones piggyback and taught the older ones Oromo games. John followed Negussie around incessantly, drawn like a magnet. Negussie showed him habitats of animals, and introduced him to the stealthy art of bird watching. Nests fascinated the children. In bamboo reeds, the sacklike homes of the yellow weaver birds hung head high — just right for them to be able to peep into, for a weaver suitor designed his nest's single door at the bottom, not the top.

In the dry season the playmates roamed the area, balanced themselves on a log over the stream, and played in the woods on the other side. During the small and bigger rains that ran from March to September, they sloshed in the mud — the Coleman kids in boots that nicked their shins and the Ethiopian children barefoot and untroubled by the complications of wash day. Their mothers simply soaped and rinsed by the stream and hung clothes on plants or fences. Bea Coleman laboriously heated water on the back of a wood stove, manually operated a hand agitator and wringer, and, between rain showers, hung the embarrassingly long string of clothes out on a line.

When it rained, Monopoly games sometimes went on for days of kingdom building. Being older, Negussie could win most of the time. He'd hide hundred-dollar bills and then plead poverty. The Coleman kids would take pity on him and let him pass their property without paying. Then later, when he owned a set of green houses, he would find his money and buy red hotels! He was such fun that even losing to him was enjoyable.

"He's always around our home, yet at meal times, he seems to tactfully disappear," Bea told out-of-town visitors, chuckling. When an Ethiopian teacher nicknamed him "the Minister of the Interior," the Colemans realized they'd best be careful not to show favoritism.

In a tribal society, foreigners had to be especially careful to guard against making cultural errors that would confuse or mislead people whose customs the Westerners did not know or understand. Negussie often explained some usage to the Colemans and advised them in cultural matters. "He just seems to have an old man's head on his young shoulders," Bea would say, shaking her curly blond head. Bea once purchased a big round woven Ethiopian basket with a lid, in which she placed her mending. In the evening she would sit by the fireplace sewing, but she began to notice that Oromos who came to visit in their home would eye that basket suspiciously. She asked Negussie why, and he explained that it was the type of basket used by the fertility cult, where they stored the milk of the fertility cow and annually had special ceremonies to guarantee fertility for their women and livestock. Alas, the basket had to go.

Soft-spoken Murray managed the station, visited churches, and encouraged local believers in various ways. Bea's day-today life was also full. Caring for a home required painstaking efforts to keep the family clean, clothed, and fed from a garden. But she taught classes at the school and in the neighborhood as well. Marianne was born their second year there, joining Danny at home, while John and Sharon had to go off to boarding school in the capital much of the time. At the mission school, the two older children found themselves lost among a hundred and fifty "MKs" — missionary kids — all struggling consciously or subconsciously with the loneliness of separation from their parents. John also missed his friend Negussie keenly.

A lively young German nurse named Chris Ott had come to work at the clinic, and she took a keen interest in the local youth. Chris taught Negussie's Sunday morning class and she allowed him to help teach younger children. She saw that he was prepared to be grounded in the Scriptures. Negussie yearned to have his own copy of the Bible. Local families hardly owned a book or had the cash to buy one. Their wealth was "banked" simply in cattle. She decided to offer an Amharic Bible to any student who would memorize two hundred Bible verses. Week by week he would repeat an amazing number of verses word-perfectly to Chris. In six short weeks he had won his Bible!

When he was about fifteen, Negussie was among the first group of young people from the mission to be prepared for baptism. They first were examined by elders from the Chebo church up in the hills, the men who subsequently baptized them and extended to them their first communion. It was a quiet affair, perhaps hardly noticed by Negussie's family. As yet, there were few adult believers near the mission station. "Believers" was the term used to differentiate the "new church" community, in contrast to the ancient Orthodox Church adherents. This was one time when Negussie was probably fortunate to be overlooked in the home, since traditional Orthodox people were suspicious of adult baptism.

There came a day, however, when Negussie was certainly not overlooked. His father came searching for him very specifically.

"Where's Negussie?" Ato Kumbi demanded as he stormed to the Coleman's door. "Tell me where he is!" Ato Kumbi seemed desperate and furious. The Colemans hadn't seen Negussie for a day or two and really didn't know. Much later, they finally pieced together the story. Weeks before, Negussie's birth mother, who lived some five or six hours walk from the clinic, had come all the way to the nurse at Obi because she was troubled by vaginal bleeding. Chris told her she needed either surgical repair or a hysterectomy. Chris and the Colemans had begged Ato Kumbi then to let them take her to Addis for help. He flatly refused and could not be budged. Negussie knew little of all this, for he had grown up in the other wife's compound.

Kumbi's outburst had happened during Christmas vacation. Not until after the vacation did the Colemans learn what had happened to Negussie. They discovered that the head of the area's witch doctors had accused Negussie's mother of insulting him. Consequently, he announced that he had put a curse on her. Then he demanded that Ato Kumbi come with money and a large ox for a sacrifice, bringing the whole immediate family. Negussie was nowhere to be found. Finally the family felt forced to make the sacrifice, even without him. After Christmas, Negussie turned up again. It seemed he had sought the advice of two Christian teachers who taught at Obi, and they had taken him home with them to Saja, far down the road toward Jimma, so he would not have to attend the pagan ceremony. Ato Kumbi's wife remained untreated and eventually, in spite of the animal sacrifice to reverse the curse, she did die. Although Negussie was not close to his birth mother, her death could not fail to sadden him.

Negussie had heartaches in these years, but he was seeing a wider world than his father yet could. The new Christian movement was like "new wine being poured into old wineskins," as

Jesus had put it.   The stretch was threatening for the tightly defined Ethiopian Orthodox community.

For instance, Negussie witnessed an unprecedented event. The mission-related "new church" leaders from all over Ethiopia chose Wolisso for their association's annual meeting. For four days in February, forty Ethiopians and twenty missionaries came and met day and night in a simple mud-walled and tin-roofed church. Wider gatherings of local Christians were held concurrently in an open field where people sat on the ground, shaded by temporarily erected arbors made of eucalyptus poles overlaid with leafy branches. The crowd sang and prayed and ate together. For hours, people sat in rapt attention, listening to the Word of God. As dusk came, people dispersed and leaders conducted church business late into the night.

But the wonder of it all to Negussie was the joyful camaraderie of such widely varying people — people from tribes that had stolen each other's cattle, burned each other's homes, and murdered each other for centuries. There were people from the heartland tribes of Hadiya, Kambatta, Wallamo, and Gedeo; men from Bale in the east; Kaffa believers from the west; and Gamo Gofans from deep in the southlands that stretched to the Kenyan border. They were from all sorts of ethnic groups and were all shades of color. Tribes and "shades" are a basis for prejudice in nearly all societies. Wonder of wonders, these believers who knew themselves to be "one in Christ" were dipping their *injera* into the same dish of *wut*, and embracing one another in heartfelt unity. Most of them were first or second generation Christians, people "in their first love" of the Savior who, they testified, "had brought them out of darkness into His marvelous light." Additionally, Negussie witnessed the sight of all these Ethiopians accepting foreigners. Foreigners were deeply suspect to most Ethiopians. The visiting participants all lived in Ethiopia, but they'd come from Europe and North America, Australia and New Zealand. The gathering constituted a many-splendored miracle that deeply touched each one there as they witnessed the unity that God can give — not only as stated on the Bible's written page, but walking in flesh.

Such fellowship stirred Negussie's heart. He made himself more and more available to assist the missionaries. Language was one skill he could offer. Missionaries were required to study Amharic, Ethiopia's language of business and education, before being located "down country." After learning Amharic, foreigners faced the challenge of the local tribal language next. In the Wolisso area, that meant Shoa Oromo. Negussie helped the Colemans and the foreign nurse and teacher to develop their Amharic and learn equivalent Oromo words. Meanwhile, he picked up their English.

Bea had a gift for language, which stood her in good stead as she went around teaching. This lithe little woman would make her way over rocky soil and muddy roads, sometimes riding a horse or mule to more distant points. Negussie's aid as a guide and interpreter proved invaluable. In turn, he was soon using English better than any of the other local youth. This acquisition of English would become a stepping stone, since English was Ethiopia's language of higher education. Schools taught English as a foreign language from third to sixth grades, and then used English as the medium of instruction thereafter.

Even though the Orthodox Church was not happy about it, the Emperor had allowed missions to enter Ethiopia even before the Italian invasion in 1937 — largely, it seemed, for the schools, hospitals, and clinics they brought. The early language school and then clinic and school built at Obi station were one example. Obi was part of a network of outreach sponsored by the Sudan Interior Mission (SIM) which had pioneered in Ethiopia in 1927. Back then, "the Soudan" meant the belt below the African Sahara. Among the mission's early leadership in Ethiopia was an American Presbyterian medical doctor named Lambie, who became a close friend and consultant of Haile Selassie. Dr. Lambie eventually helped set up the country's educational system.

In the early days, the mission first located a language school in Wolisso town, before they built Obi station. The business community accepted the foreigners better than the ecclesiastical establishment did. Wolisso was well known for a hotel with hot mineral springs. In the Coleman's time of leadership at Obi, a helpful trade developed. On Monday afternoons, the student body marched into town and swam in the hotel's pool free. In return, hotel employees got free treatment at the mission clinic. Negussie's schoolmates enjoyed countless hours of fun at that pool and whenever they were home, the Coleman kids joined in.

During the academic year, the Colemans' older children were away long months with only the preschoolers left at home. During vacations, John and Negussie picked up where they left off, bonding ever more firmly. Again they would roam the woods together, chattering constantly, or stop breathless, sharing a thrilling encounter with some wild creature.   In the evenings they would bid each other goodnight by the stile under the ancient *zigabah* , an indigenous tree that soared above the mission compound and neighboring homes. They would drag out their parting as long as they could.   Moonlight outlined the grass peaks of round huts and threw rippling highlights on the tin roofs of the station's school, clinic, and houses, the peaceful scene that comprised their shared world.

Periodically, when John would leave for boarding school or the family would depart for furlough, the friends poignantly acted out their "David-and-Jonathan" relationship through the exchanging of gifts — a rare coin or some other treasure. When the separation was over, they would continue to dream together, sharing hopes and ambitions, eagerly wondering, "What do our lives hold in store?"

CAMARADERIE
AND CONFLICT

A thunderbolt cracked through the skies, shook the ground, and rumbled across the earth. Negussie stirred in his deep sleep as the reverberations echoed onward toward the hills. Rain poured down on the thatched-roofed compound. Inside the hut, Negussie pulled his thick cotton *gabi* (heavy shawl) more closely around himself. As he dozed between volleys, the pelting rain abated, toned down to patters, and finally just dripped. A lone bird chirped. Others soon chimed in. An embarrassed rooster hurriedly crowed.

Negussie rose and stretched. Dodging a puddle on the dirt floor, he unbarred the cow and a couple of sheep and goats from their portion of the hut and turned them outside to graze in drenched grass. Negussie's stepmother depended upon him to do much in the absence of her husband, which was most of the time. There were chores for Negussie to do before *ding-ding-ding* sounded out from the school to announce class time. In the chilly morning, he looked forward to the warm camaraderie he was enjoying in school. Scattered among the students were young people who had chosen to confess Jesus the Christ as their Lord. Every day their eyes met across the desks, confirming their shared identity.

Many had been attracted to Christ through traveling teachers who came to Wolisso periodically to lead Christian confer-

ences. One such national evangelist was Ato Kaydamo, a
Kambattan from Hosanna, a city many kilometers south of
Wolisso. A tall, broad-shouldered man with tremendous speaking gifts, Kaydamo had a passionate relationship with the Lord.
The vitality of the man's faith was contagious. His twinkling
eyes, staccato wit, and skillful applications made his messages
unforgettable. Ato Kaydamo counseled young believers between
meetings. His modeling would be seen later in these young
people's lives. Counseling was a role the young Negussie was
increasingly being asked to exercise. It seemed to be his gift.

Every Sunday Mrs. Coleman taught the local youth from the
Bible. Bibles were rare and precious. Unlike local Orthodox
Christians, evangelicals did all they could to encourage lay people
to read the Scriptures. Negussie had earned his Bible just as quickly
as the nurse and Mrs. Coleman had made them available. Others
students who became part of this fellowship of believers were
working on memorizing their two hundred verses to procure their
own. Bea heard their verses on Saturday mornings. Most were
young men, but a few girls were active believers in Jesus as well.

One of Negussie's classmates was a fellow named Tesfaye,
who lived a mile or so up in the hills toward Addis. Tesfaye was
taller than most of the fellows and had a gracious way about him.
Negussie bonded with him as he too gave keen attention when
Bea took the students through Acts and Philippians and other
books of their choice.

In the book of Acts, they met the first-century Ethiopian official who had visited Jerusalem. In his chariot on the trip home,
the man had been reading the Messianic passage in Isaiah 53
when God sent Philip to his side. On learning that "the lamb" of
that passage was Jesus of Nazareth, the Ethiopian asked Philip,
"What is to prevent my being baptized?" Many of the students
were asking the same question.

Public adult baptism was becoming no small matter in Ethiopian society, centuries after this biblical account, for a metamorphosis had taken place. Historically, three hundred years after

that Ethiopian's baptism in the first century A.D., King Ezana was converted and committed his whole Ethiopian kingdom to being "Christian." That was about the time of Constantine. Families came to expect their children to continue in the household of faith, so infant baptism became the practice of the realm. Seventeen centuries later, this was unquestioned as the mode of baptism for most Ethiopians.

In contrast, the missionaries began their work among animists in the south, where individuals were coming out of an animistic society as adults, and one by one. The foreigners wanted these new believers to have a way of marking their conversion and commitment. But when the two cultures intertwined, public baptism of an adult threatened both the animistic and Orthodox communities, which sometimes overlapped. On the one hand, the animists lived in constant fear of upsetting the precarious balance of the community. They relied heavily upon witch doctors that performed sacrifices to appease Satan or the spirits, costly sacrifices thought to protect people from torment, illness, childlessness, or drought. For an animist to be baptized a Christian signaled a challenge to all these practices. On the other hand, for an Orthodox adult to be baptized seemed an offense to the traditions of that community. Had not Orthodox people already been baptized as infants? Was not the Church into which they had been baptized their ark of salvation? So this baptism issue was no small matter for individuals or the community.

In the new churches it was the custom to defer baptism until new Christians had developed a firm biblical base. The Colemans carefully shepherded their students even after they left the Obi school, which only went through fourth grade in the early days. Students had to go into Wolisso to a town school from fifth grade on. Negussie and some of the others rented a room together. Their quarters were simple. Negussie once mentioned to John the difficulty of having to use candles to study by at night. The Coleman kids starting saving all their household stubs, melted them, and lovingly presented Negussie with one huge candle. They were delighted to hear how long it lasted.

Murray went in weekly to meet with the group and lead them in Bible study. Finally a time was set for their baptism. It happened that John was to be home from Bingham Academy on the appointed date, and so he asked to be baptized with Tesfaye and these friends he'd grown up around, although John was not quite twelve.

For this unusual event, believers in the area wended their way with the candidates down to the Jersa River, which flowed close to Negussie's home. The community looked much as the crowd at the Jordan River might have looked the day of Jesus' baptism, all dressed in white cotton clothing with head shawls, similar to Old Testament times, for such garb was still typical of Ethiopia. And as each went under the water between two elders, they publicly identified themselves as Christians "in the name of the Father, the Son, and the Holy Spirit." As each walked up the bank, dripping and deeply moved, the fellowship welcomed the new member with the trilled *ililta* (joy cry). Afterwards, the believers assembled to take the Lord's Supper, obedient to their Lord's directive to "do this in remembrance of me, until I come."

Standing among the already baptized believers, Negussie was deeply moved to share this significant baptism and communion with John and Tesfaye and many of his closest friends, one of whom had come to school from a distance and turned out to actually be a relative. Of course Bea and Murray were thrilled. They took a picture that they were destined to treasure. There was their son among the young Ethiopians. There was tall Tesfaye smiling, dressed in a worn sweater, jeans, and running shoes. Each had a story, and each would continue to intersect with the Colemans' lives as they matured. Joy and thanksgiving marked the unforgettable day.

Yet for some of the community, this outrageous baptism seemed foreign, unforgivable. The family of one student threw him out of their house.

SCATTERING

A familiar Land Rover pulled into the Colemans' yard and out hopped Ted Veer, a trim young man with a crew cut and a deep voice that invited confidence. Ted was an American and an old friend of the Colemans. He sometimes dropped in as he traveled back and forth on the Jimma Road. They'd known him during his years at Saja station before he was given a new assignment in Jimma, the hub of the Kaffa province. Ted was now the enthusiastic principal of Grace Bible Institute, an upper-level school the mission had recently founded for students advanced enough to be taught in English.

Ted was always looking for promising students, and among Negussie's group, one dedicated and especially brilliant fellow stood out. He was the slight young man with whom John had been baptized, the one Negussie had found to be his relative. Ted talked with him, and eventually the lad began studies at Jimma. One weekend when a car was traveling to Jimma, Negussie got a ride to visit him at GBI. There Negussie was introduced to a wider world. Jimma was a big center amid a Muslim population. The mission's school flanked the Missionary Aviation Fellowship property. MAF maintained a hub base at Jimma to serve remote stations in the mountains and deserts of Ethiopia's rugged southwest. Negussie met well-educated young people who could use English as a medium, students from all over Ethiopia, including Eritrea, in spite of that province's guerrilla war of secession. He made the acquaintance of a spirited young Eritrean named Mesghina, a man he'd be surprised to meet in other circumstances one day. Ato Tekle, Ted Veer's co-worker from Saja, was one of the older people studying there to be equipped for national church leadership in the future. He was among the married students. A couple of students had come over from Sudan, and there were a few women who came to study at GBI, among them, one of Negussie's Wolisso classmates.

And so it was that in the seventies, Negussie's old friends were beginning to scatter. Along with maturity came new challenges, challenges that led them down separate paths.

When Tesfaye had finished eleventh grade in the town school, he was offered a place in the military college at Harrar, the Emperor's town in the eastern part of the country. His old friends were reluctant to see him drawn into the military world, but drawn he was. Being an officer in the military looked bright to him at that stage. He could not yet picture the horrors of war and famine in the north, which would eventually surround him.

Meanwhile, Ato Kaydamo had moved to Addis and wasn't doing as much itinerant teaching at Wolisso as he had before. The church to which he'd been called was not one of the many traditional Ethiopian Orthodox churches which dotted the city and had ancient roots, but one of those that had emerged out of the "new churches" movement. Sometimes they were called "Protestants." That term was shorn of its European historical content in Ethiopia. There, a Protestant simply meant a Christian who was "neither Orthodox nor Catholic," the two historically accepted forms.

Years after his initial interview in Addis, Ato Kaydamo used to tell about his country-boy struggle with going to be "looked over" in the capital. It was his habit to tell amusing stories, sometimes about his own foibles, as a vehicle for teaching some principle. When Ato Kaydamo had become comfortable in the city church, the country preacher used to quip, "Come to hear the preacher who never learned!" GBI hadn't existed in his youth. His schooling included little English "learning," but had been taught in "down-country Amharic," which sounded unlearned to the Amhara ear. He'd tell how, when he was invited to candidate in Addis, he had just one suit to his name. It was a khaki one made by a roadside tailor in Hosanna. He got it all pressed, but when he arrived in Addis in the cool season, he found men to be wearing stylish wool suits. He tried to put his best foot forward, but could not help speaking with a down-country Kambattan accent, not like an Amhara with impeccable Amharic. People snickered during the first few minutes of the candidate's message, until the solidness of the content and dynamism of his preaching began to dawn on them. He soon won their hearts.

It was John's departure that was the most poignant loss for Negussie. John had to leave Ethiopia with his family for their furlough and then remain in Canada to finish high school since the mission school in Addis did not extend through the upper grades. Murray and Bea helped him settle in during his first year, but he was to remain there alone in a Christian boarding school after they left. During this time, the two young men began bridging the gap between them through letters. Thin blue one-page airforms began to go back and forth. Most Ethiopians Negussie's age could not use English well enough to correspond, but Negussie could, even though his wording was a bit broken and betrayed an occasional hazy understanding of idioms. His November 1972 airform began:

> Dear Johnny, ...I'm very glad and thankful about your lovely letter which I had last time. Even if we don't have a chance to see face to face here on earth, for we contact through letter every time, I don't worry much like I used to have. Still I'll have hope of your coming back to Ethiopia once upon a time which is not very far. I'm still looking to that day. Don't you think?

He told of his classes, students who had believed, the seasonal changes, and even teased about his changes: "I hope if you look at me you may see different appearance. I've nice clothes and a watch. You may say you've grown tall and fat maybe." The last third of the airform's limited space, he explained, he saved to write to "Mom and Dad." It was in beautiful Amharic script and was addressed formally to "Mr. and Mrs. Coleman."

The next letter said John's answer had revived him, but expressed the keen pain of separation:

> ...Yes! It should be true, for I love you and respect you as one of my relatives and it is true also you are my spiritual relative... How it'll be wonderful if I could be alive to see you! Sometimes when I think that you'll not be back this year to Ethiopia, I do feel that I lost a great thing in my life. What will I feel when I'll go to the airport to receive Mom and Dad, Danny and Marianne, but couldn't see you and Sharon?

This time, Negussie added a special note in English to John's younger brother Danny, including a little joke about hockey in snowy Canada and swimming in Wolisso's hot springs:

> Be happy, for you will come to your warm weather country after a few months. Then rather than play hockey in left wing, you will swim in the pool with me to the left wing (side) okay?

When they got back to Ethiopia, the Colemans were reassigned to Addis, not to Wolisso. Negussie was the one feeling left behind at Obi, but he made a change, too. He was gifted as a teacher, and since Ethiopians often contributed a year as instructors out in a "bush" school after they reached a certain standard, Negussie earnestly gave his year of service at an isolated area with few educational advantages.

He then was given a staff position at his old school at Obi, now led by a new principal, Ato Tekle Wolde Giorgos. Negussie had known him previously, for Tekle was from Saja, where Negussie had spent that Christmas vacation when the witch doctor had demanded the pagan sacrifices. The new principal had also studied at GBI, where Negussie had met him again when visiting the school. Tekle was a kindly, short man with a furrowed brow and alert eyes. He was one of the older married men who was a leader in the national church. Living and working side by side with Ato Tekle at Obi, Negussie came to know and love his large family, and even taught his principal's daughter in third grade.

When the Colemans did an assignment at Shashamane Leprosarium in Arussi territory, they invited Negussie to come for a two-week rest from his work that summer of 1974. The trip was an eye-opening exposure to a whole new culture. The Arusi wore leather clothing and seemed to be a fierce people who did not receive outsiders kindly. Dan and Marianne were home from boarding school in Addis. What a reunion it was! By day they all enjoyed the Rift Valley lakes, and at night they played games and looked at slides from Canada, getting a better idea of John and Sharon's surroundings. They even heard John's voice on a tape and Negussie's heart burned within him. He wrote John pages that week to be included in an envelope the Colemans were sending to Canada.

Back in Wolisso, each week Negussie went eagerly to the post office. Few down-country people got mail. He pored over every word of John's letters and wrote back as an older brother. One 1974 letter said:

> It is such a long time since we've stayed apart. Even though, we are still together before our heavenly Father. For we dwell before One Father and have shared from the same spiritual food... John! I am praising the Lord about your Christian life. Your

great desire to follow Jesus... Yes, my beloved
friend, it is wonderful to practice the way of CROSS
in young stage. When you're growing physically,
the spiritual growth will also follow. In the past
time, we see that in the Bible God called David,
Samuel, and in the N.T. Mark started to follow Jesus
when he was very young. God has a great work for
us and this is why he called us during our young
stage.

They wrote about their lives and hopes. Negussie had always been highly patriotic and he wrote of his opportunity now
to serve in his country's educational development. He was aware
of new political winds blowing in the capital. "It isn't stable
yet," he wrote, "but I hope it'll be over and will be peaceful very
soon...We all Ethiopians are ready to serve our nation according
to God's will."

John hardly knew how to explain to an Ethiopian his
struggles as a displaced teen in Canada. Little things would
send a wave of loneliness through him — the aroma of a kero-
sene lamp, a mountain vista, the bray of a donkey. A sense of
estrangement would sweep over him as he tried to live with
roommates who weren't "foreigners." He felt himself to be the
foreigner now, even if his passport said "Canadian." Had he not
been born in Ethiopia? He felt Ethiopian, regardless of his
skin.

Seeing each other again was their treasured hope. In a letter that year, Negussie mentioned the coming of the rains, after
the dry months, and reminisced:

How good to see when all things are green... If you
remember this is the time when we used to go across
the river and roll over the green pasture. I do remember when we used to go for a walk along the
Jersa River specially to a clean spring where I wash
my clothes. What shall I say? Now it seems to me

that we're together and talking. How it is wonderful to have you with me or I with you and live together and serve the Lord! Oh! Johnny I'd like to see you!!! I know that you really love me from your heart and look at me as one of your family member and so do I. You're my real brother that I got you through Christ and your family too. You know? Many Ethiopian people also understood and even look me as your family representative. Last news - I've been chosen as one of the Elders of the church at Obi. Please pray for me that I'll serve the Lord's Church faithfully before Him. Ps. 85:8 for you and me. Goodbye! Love, Negussie.

The relative of Negussie's who had been among the Wolisso comrades wrote to John occasionally. His letters helped fill in the picture of what was happening to their friends. In early October of 1974 he wrote:

Negussie will go tomorrow to Asmara for Teacher Training. I'd like to go to night school and work in the day time this coming year, but I don't know if there will be school this year for high school students because of the government change which took place in Ethiopia. The new government set a plan that all the students above 10th grade should go to the countryside and teach the people who don't know what the government means and teach them to read and write. I don't know what will happen. But I'm happy because I work for a different kingdom.

None of them could have known what cataclysmic changes the Ethiopian kingdom was about to experience. Their primary Kingdom, however, remained firm.

STORM CLOUDS IN
THE NORTH

"John, you've got to do something!"

John Cumbers moved the phone farther from his ear. Mr. Cumbers, Field Director of SIM in Ethiopia, was used to Dr. Schmoll's German accent and choleric nature, but the man seemed beside himself today. He was calling from the mission hospital and leprosarium that he administered up north in Dessie. His high pitched staccato voice was both urgent and shaken.

"I've seen terrible sights in eastern Wollo! We have discovered hundreds of people starving, and there are already dozens dying every day. Why hasn't there been any government report of this famine?" He cut John off, hardly waiting for an answer. "People are lying beside the road. They don't even have the strength to approach the vehicles that pass by!"

Before the outraged doctor slammed down the receiver, John had promised to get some kind of famine relief organized.

Mr. Cumbers stood at his office window overlooking a busy Addis intersection. His tall, thin frame sagged as he faced what might be coming. He'd repeatedly driven the long road north from Addis to Asmara, Eritrea's capital, stopping for the night midway at the hospital in Dessie. Drought was regularly a threat in that dry highland terrain, but this year's lack of rain was becoming disastrous. He sighed. One more thing to add to the pile of mission projects that already taxed his limited staff and resources. As the head of SIM, he had to oversee the work of over 200 missionaries (including the Obi station down at Wolisso). There were mission schools to administer (like the one Negussie had attended); Grace Bible institute (where Ato Tekle had trained); and the mission press (where the Colemans were working). There were clinics and hospitals around the country, not only the one where Dr. Schmoll worked at Dessie, but others, too. There were agricultural projects and well drilling rigs and construction crews. And now this! He could not know that the famine would soon escalate to such a proportion as to draw in funds and relief workers from all over the world.

Already the north was struggling with the Eritrean insurgency, which was a worry in itself. Mission workers up there were becoming enmeshed in the tensions of guerrilla warfare, bombing, injuries, and kidnappings. John Cumbers was more conversant with the Eritrean struggle than most foreigners because of having worked in Asmara during his pre-mission days. In fact, soon after he had left the British Royal Air Force in 1945, he had come to Eritrea to help train air traffic controllers for the fledgling airfield at Asmara.

In Asmara he met other Christians at Asmara's Gospel Center, including the widow of a young missionary doctor who had died after contracting hepatitis from a patient's autopsy. Eventually he had married Naomi and joined her mission. After serving one term in the south and one in the north, John moved into the role of Field Director.

And so it was that his family was living at "HQ," the mission's headquarters, on a fourth-of-a-block property near downtown Addis. On his office wall hung a map of Ethiopia with pins marking the location of all the stations he was responsible to direct. Most of them were in the south, for that was the "heathen" area in which the Emperor had invited missions to work.

Soon the famine would be bringing a whole new fleet of short-term volunteers into the north. The doctor had glimpsed only the tip of the iceberg. The government could no longer keep the starving a secret after a BBC documentary broke and shocked the world. When it was over, the famine of 1973 would be reported to have left more than 100,000 dead.

Concurrent with this natural calamity which sent expatriates north, southern Ethiopians were being pushed northward too, for political reasons. They were being rounded up in marketplaces and sent off to fight against the Eritrean secessionists. That ethnic conflict was affecting the whole country. It strained once-peaceful relationships, pitting Eritreans and Ethiopians against one another wherever they coexisted.

Students at Grace Bible Institute felt the rupture way out in Jimma. They became more and more nervous as Eritrean friends in Jimma town simply disappeared, taken from their homes at night. Mesghina, one of those GBI students Negussie had met while visiting GBI, graduated and went north to Eritrea, thankful to be alive and free.

That did not solve an Eritrean's problem, however. What seemed a safe move north for Eritreans could prove as dangerous to life and limb as being in the south, for at home everyone knew them or their relatives, and all able-bodied youth, male and sometimes female, were expected to join "the Front." Which front was a dilemma. Two groups struggled for supremacy, the ELF (Eritrean Liberation Front) and the EPLF (Eritrean Peoples' Liberation Front). The first group was composed primarily of lowlanders, the second of highlanders. Even though the region was small, Eritrea comprised vastly different landforms, languages, and cultures. Cultural roots were different, and they competed. Both fronts tried to outdo each other in applying Marxist doctrine and conscripting fighters

As both fronts' brothers and sisters and fathers and friends were killed in the field, those who survived grew increasingly committed to their not having died in vain. Earnest Christians whose allegiance was to the Prince of Peace found themselves in a vulnerable position. Killing was repugnant to people who knew themselves to be just one among the "all" for whom Christ had given His life, all equally loved and equally precious to Him. Furthermore, those who had shared friendships with a wide spectrum of Christians had personally experienced the unity shared by believers, regardless of ethnic background.

On the other hand, freedom fighters living in the field of war had been indoctrinated with Marxist philosophy, to which the doctrine of love was anathema. "This gun is my god," a guerrilla growled at one believer who tried to explain the reason for his reticence to kill, "and I will level it at you if I hear more of your God talk!"

In the midst of this growing instability, Negussie's educational opportunity arrived, and to his surprise, it meant going to Eritrea! As it happened, officials assigned him to the Teachers Training Institute located in Asmara. *What an adventure, to get to go to Eritrea,* he must have thought, *and yet, is it safe to even try?*

The trip was an experience. He was crammed into a crowded bus filled with northerners — mostly Eritreans — who coldly eyed him and three other students from Shoa Province. Above, baggage was piled high, and inside, chickens squawked in cages and perishables in baskets diffused their various odors into the already stifling air. Sometimes a threatening surge of speed broke the boredom of rumbling along hour after hour. Bus drivers frequently raced with their competitors as if oblivious to the safety of their customers. Negussie prayed as they careened along the twisting Asmara road. It threaded over dramatic mountain passes and down through deep gorges. Occasionally the bus made a quick "rest stop" in some lonely stretch of road where men and women could fan out on each side of the bus.

As the vehicle moved northward, Negussie noticed the soil became more and more rocky and the altitude increased. The sun sets quickly that near the equator, and the air turns brisk at such altitudes. He wrapped himself in his white *gabi* when the chill came on.

The second day, the weary travelers passed the halfway point at Dessie, from which the doctor had called John Cumbers in Addis. Negussie was unprepared for the shock of face-to-face confrontation with pitiful bands of people who stood along the roadside. When the bus stopped, they reached emaciated arms up to the windows, their sunken eyes pleading, too weak to speak. *What can I do?* Negussie wondered. He had only some grain in his pocket. The extent of the suffering staggered him. *Why did we not even hear of this in Wolisso?* he wondered. Having been an oddly shaped child who barely survived himself, he shuddered as he studied the spindly children who were carried by desperate mothers. The babies had sticklike arms and legs poking out of swollen torsos. The red tinge of their hair betrayed *kwashiorkor*, one of the stages of starvation. Between the nightmare stops, Negussie closed his eyes, but the faces, the bodies, the eyes rose up before him, indelibly inscribed. What could be done?

Weary of travel and shaken by the specters he'd seen, Negussie longed for the groaning bus to finish the long, twisting climb to the city of Asmara. Fog sometimes cut off the capital from the awful sights below.

Asmara was the Eritrean seat of government and the crown city of the province. It enjoyed invigorating temperatures, for it was perched high on the escarpment that plunged into desert lowlands bordered by the Red Sea. From Asmara, a breathtaking road snaked down through the clouds to Massawa. Reluctance to lose the Massawa and Assab seaports was a major factor in Ethiopia's battle against Eritrea's secession.

Because Eritrea had fallen into the hands of Italy in the late 1800's, she had undergone a certain Romanization, especially in roads, training, and architecture. Ethiopia had first defeated the Italians in 1896 at the famous battle of Adowa, but Eritrea remained an Italian colony. Again they were driven out with the help of the British, after Italy's five-year occupation of Ethiopia ending in 1941. According to post-World War II settlements, in 1952 Eritrea was given a measure of self-rule under federation to Ethiopia. But in 1962, the Emperor unilaterally annexed the area and made it an integral province of Ethiopia. From then on, Eritrean dissidents and guerrillas in the field waged a secessionist battle.

When Negussie arrived at the Teachers Training Institute in Asmara in the mid-seventies, anti-government guerrilla activity seethed around the city. Yet there at the region's heart, the "enemy's" Ethiopian Army and Air Base was firmly ensconced. In the countryside, Eritreans were taken up with struggles among their own political factions. But of these matters, Negussie said nothing in his letters to John. Perhaps an Ethiopian knew he dared not, or perhaps his focus was quite elsewhere. "I can serve the Lord here in Asmara also" he wrote.

Ironically, the brightest spot of Negussie's schooling experience in Asmara was the fellowship he discovered at the mission's Youth Center, which proved to be a strange oasis from the war. A collection of potential enemies came together there — Eritrean city dwellers, TTI students from all around Ethiopia, Ethiopian military men from the base, and even an occasional Eritrean guerrilla. At the Center, they all could experience contact with each other as people to enjoy rather than as positions to defend. Christ had "broken down the dividing wall of hostility," as the Apostle Paul put it.

Negussie was surprised to run into Mesghina, the Eritrean student who had left GBI during those tense days. By now, Mesghina was directing an orphanage in Dekemhare, around thirty-five kilometers out of Asmara. The mission's Youth Center in Asmara was a favorite place for the teenage Dekemhare orphans to visit on weekends. Eritrea's youth faced early conscription. Life was serious and visiting the Center gave them a place of temporary refuge.

Another cluster of young men who dropped into the Center came from the Ethiopian Air Force Base about seven kilometers outside of the city. Measured politically by Eritreans, these men would have been seen as "the enemy." But on Friday nights a bunch of the soldiers at the Base would pile into a van and head for the Center. The various groups would talk together till the wee hours of the morning. At times, teams from the Center, including even the Air Force men, would travel out to Dekemhare's orphanage for a weekend of camp-type meetings, bringing teaching, drama, and games.

Among those Ethiopian servicemen touched by the Center were three master sergeants from Negussie's own Shoa region in the center of the country. Solomon, Girma, and Teshome were all in their early twenties and unmarried, and had been trained as technicians at the Ethiopian Air Force headquarters in Debre Zeit, just south of Addis. They listened carefully as a Canadian missionary and Eritrean leaders taught from the Scriptures and talked about the Lord Jesus. Teshome was the first of the trio to give himself to Christ. Solomon and Girma also soon awoke to a personal relationship with the Savior. The three began to study the Scriptures and develop unusually warm hearts toward their Lord. They felt that their fellow servicemen needed what they had discovered in the living Christ. Jesus told his disciples they were to become "fishers of men." These three became skilled fishermen who drew many servicemen into the safe net of Christ's love, despite Marxist doctrine in the military.

Fellowship at the Center was warm, but the Marxist atmosphere at the Air Base could be cold toward soldiers who were open about faith. For a man to expose himself as Christian in the military often meant being accused, harassed, and cut out of promotions and extra benefits. Nevertheless, Solomon, Girma, and Teshome accepted the challenge. "We have to pay the price for our Lord's service," Teshome would insist, unmoved by intimidation.

Negussie was strengthened, seeing such commitment. And they, with their strained nerves, were blessed by his sunny disposition. At some point Negussie picked up guitar playing, and he loved to lead joyful songs of praise. They sang along with him. Little did they know that soon he would be strumming other songs, songs of suffering.

REVOLUTION!

John Coleman's heart skipped a beat when the news reached Canada. *What's happening to Dad and Mom in Addis?* he wondered. On Ethiopian New Year's Day — which had been celebrated half a century under Haile Selassie's rule — the unthinkable had happened. That night, the ruling group, known as "the *Derg*" made an international announcement. The Emperor had been deposed! The 1955 Constitution had been revoked. Parliament had been dissolved. The ancient Solomonic dynasty, despite its historical credentials, had come to an end.

In Addis, neither expatriates nor nationals could fathom what had occurred. John Cumbers' diary recorded that fateful September 12, 1974 :

> A Volkswagen Bug pulled up outside the gates of the Imperial Palace in Addis Ababa. Three army officers entered the Emperor's study and told him he was to accompany them. As they approached the little car, one of them tipped up the front seat and motioned to the Emperor. Haile Selassie the First, King of Kings and Conquering Lion of the Tribe of Judah, accustomed to Rolls Royce treatment, climbed into the back seat of the bug and made his journey into ignominy.

John Cumbers wondered how it could have happened. For some time the mission staff had been aware of unrest, particularly in the student population of Ethiopia. At Bingham Academy, the school his son and daughter attended along with other missionary children, the faculty had felt compelled to create a secret riot shelter — a tunnel underneath the main building. The university and even high school students in Addis seemed to be protesting all the time — asking for land reforms, for more representative government, for changes in the educational system and the like. But John had dismissed them as "just students." Now it seemed they were at the very heart of the revolution. Even though the Emperor had championed the education they were enjoying, his inattention to their recurrent demands had brought forth a harvest of revolt. The fact that the Emperor's successor was not installed, not even decided upon, had rankled students who were growing too informed and too determined to be put off.

Students were playing a larger role than even they themselves realized. Historian Bahru Zewde would later observe that "despite the growing intensity of the confrontation, the outbreak of the Ethiopian Revolution in 1974 caught both the regime and the students unawares. The regime had scarcely thought the end was so near. The students, their years of opposition notwithstanding, had not yet formulated a clear and viable alternative." On the other hand, older political opportunists in high places were quietly formulating their own strategies.

One by one, in the middle of 1974, those closest to the Emperor had either been arrested or escaped from the country. On June 27, 1974, "a Committee of Equals" (the *Derg*) was announced. At first this ruling body proclaimed they would be loyal to Haile Selassie. The daily paper began to herald the banner *"Ethiopia Tikdem!"* ("Ethiopia first!") as a new rallying cry. Lt. Col. Atenafu Abate was named chairman and a certain Maj. Mengistu Haile Mariam (who eventually came out on top) was named vice-chairman of the 126-member Derg. Little was said concerning the policies of the "Committee of Equals," but observers on the outside thought the Derg showed promise of supplying reasonable direction to a peaceful transfer of power. However, questions arose when July 26th's report announced the forced resignation of the Prime Minister. New appointments followed. By August 15th, the Crown Council and its Review Commission as well as the Central Court were dissolved. The international airport was closed. On September 12th, the king was captured and a coup brought Ethiopia's ancient dynasty to an end.

Mr. Cumbers and other leaders speculated about how all this would affect Christian missions. Ethiopian church leaders were also in a quandary. In the face of this political upheaval, Pastor Kaydamo paced the floor of his Addis home. He was not unfamiliar with what had happened in communist states. The man was big in soul and labored under a deep sense of responsibility to his flock.

Kaydamo felt he had to deal personally with what he could see coming. "On October 3rd I gave myself to a day of prayer and fasting," he later testified. "But the Lord saw fit to withhold an answer from me. So I went on throughout that night in prayer, begging God to reveal to me what was the right thing to do. October 4th came and I'd still had no reply from God. As I was returning to my home, the Lord spoke to me. He reminded me of the words of the Lord Jesus Christ as He was about to be crucified. 'Not my will but Yours be done.' In a flash the Lord enabled me to say, 'Yes, Lord, if you want the prayer houses and the church to be closed down, so be it. If the Bible is to be banned, let it be so. If we are to be imprisoned, let it be so. Even if you want me to die for my faith, so be it.' After I had this word from the Lord I was filled with tremendous peace and joy. He gave me strong faith that He would protect us in whatever circumstances we found ourselves." Kaydamo said that from that day on, throughout the rest of their ordeals, he was not really anxious. Being willing to die, he was free to live.

Over and over again his flock was assailed, but Kaydamo kept grounding his people on the Rock who could withstand any storm.

The effects of the coup spread out in every direction. In the capital, students swelled with pride over bringing about change. They looked to the future with bright hopes. The sense of change brought excitement even in the church.

A whirlwind was sweeping through every social institution and across all the provinces. So far in Ethiopia proper, little evidence had appeared of the Marxist-Leninist philosophy which would eventually put pressure on Christians. Young church leaders were among those who looked to the future with excitement. Some were even chosen for leadership by the Marxists.

But soon ominous handwriting appeared on the wall. Strange things were happening. General Aman, chairman of the provisional government, an Eritrean, was killed in his home after a week of siege without surrender. That next day, November 24th — which became known as "Bloody Saturday" — the public was horrified to learn the meaning of repeated shots coming from an Addis prison early that morning. Most citizens first learned of it by radio. For example, Ted Veer happened to be traveling from GBI in Jimma to Addis that day. He had boarded a bus in the usual noisy confusion. As the crowded vehicle lumbered on to the road, people settled into their seats and began to chat, but before long the loudspeaker system was turned up to give passengers the benefit of the 7 AM radio news. A stark announcement blared out: "...fifty-nine ex-ministers, generals, and other former Haile Selassie appointees were executed today at dawn." Silence came over the bus. Passengers bowed their heads, stunned. Everything else seemed to hush in mourning, except for the grinding of gears as the bus navigated the mountain road. Details were filled in eventually. The Derg had executed the old leadership in two hours' time — military leaders, mayors, even the Emperor's grandson. All had been thrown into a mass grave at Kerchaylee Prison in the Akaki area, just a few kilometers south of the mission offices where John Cumbers worked.

The day after the executions, newspaper headlines heralded the accusations of the Provisionary Military Administrative Council against their victims. The deceased General Aman was accused of "working against the philosophy *Ethiopia Tikdem*," of " plotting against the popular movement of the people," and "trying to divide the PMAC." As for the others executed, November 27th's *Ethiopian Herald* reported their crimes as "maladministration... selling secret documents of the country to foreign agents... and attempting to disrupt the present Ethiopian popular movement."

On December 20th, Ethiopia was declared a socialist state.

Up in Eritrea the liberation forces had a new enemy, not a feudal king but a Marxist government. How strange for a Marxist face to be on "the enemy," for the Eritrean guerrillas had studied Mao too and saw themselves as Marxists. They were embittered when their past supporters, the Russians, made a calculated choice and backed Ethiopia, the bigger nation. Eritreans were puzzled, trying to figure out where they stood in this new chapter of their struggle for independence. And what should they do with Ethiopians?

The threat to the southern students at the Asmara TTI was great enough for officials to have them moved out of the capital for their own safety. By January 1975, Negussie's guarded letter to John Coleman in Canada was postmarked "Dekemhare," the town where Mesghina managed the orphanage. After learning more about the Eritrean situation through his parents, John tried to read between Negussie's lines:

> I really feel happy whenever I get a letter specially
> from you. I can also understand that your heart is
> with me and remembering me every time...There
> are many problems in Eritrea...The Eritreans don't
> like we Amhara TTI students and the military gov-

ernment took us to Dekemhare 40 kilometers away from Asmara for protection...you have great responsibility to do for me, i.e. PRAY FOR ME!!! Pray for the nation and for all the Christians in ETH...Please read Phil. 4:4-7. These words are those on which my heart rests ... My beloved friend John! I'll never forget you!! I'll reach you with my letter from where ever I'll be. I'll look for that happy day I'll see you here or on earth or heaven.

Growing pressures made that location a short-lived haven. Soon Negussie had to leave Eritrea completely, working his way southward toward Addis. Such travel was not simple. Crossing rugged mountains and treacherous rivers would be challenging to the fittest body. A lonely traveler on foot never knew when he would suddenly be confronted by an Ethiopian soldier, an Eritrean guerrilla, a nervous deserter, or a hardened bandit, not to mention wild animals or suspicious peasants. Bus tickets were expensive for an unpaid student, and bombing threatened the roads.

Negussie felt safer when he finally made it to Munz, an Orthodox area closer to Addis. Even there within Ethiopia proper, he was accused as a "*Pente*," from Pentecost, a derogatory term coined a few years before the Revolution by the Orthodox for non-Orthodox Christians. He taught at a school in Munz for a few months, but an unexpected incident left him nearly dead. Hearing the cries of a woman being beaten in the lodging where he slept, Negussie ran to the scene and begged her drunken lover to stop. Enraged, the man turned on the humpbacked stranger and beat him to the ground, injuring him so badly that Negussie had to be hospitalized.

The battered lad finally managed to reach Addis just in time for a rendezvous he'd been dreaming about for years. Like a homing pigeon, John Coleman took his break at the completion of high school in Canada to return to Ethiopia. The senior Colemans had gone home for John's graduation from high school and Sharon's from college, and afterwards all six of the family traveled to Ethiopia together.

Bea and Murray invited old Obi friends to come by their home at the Press compound where literature was produced. By now, quite an assortment of Wolisso-related people traveled through Addis or lived there. Chris Ott came, the nurse at Obi who had nurtured Negussie as a teenager. Ted Veer lived in Addis now, as did Ato Tekle and Pastor Kaydamo. John's rendezvous with Wolisso-related people was heartwarming, but most treasured was the arrival of Negussie.

Their reunion was ecstatic. What a rush of memories! They savored childhood experiences and shared some of what life had dealt them in their young adulthood. After the Colemans had him over, Negussie arranged another rendezvous.

He rented a taxi and took John and the other three "Coleman kids," all adults now, over to the gardens in the boulevard that ran between the Hilton Hotel and the old palace. They basked in a golden hour of being together again in Ethiopia. The sweet tea they shared — the simple treat Negussie could afford to host — was like nectar to their souls.

One day when John and Negussie were out alone together, they strolled up the busy Churchill Boulevard. Negussie linked his arm in John's, as is the custom between good male friends in Ethiopia. He valued John's friendship and did not hesitate to identify publicly in the natural way with his old friend. But John cringed with fear, for the Marxist ethos judged fraternization with Westerners, "the oppressors," as anti-Revolutionary. He kept expecting Negussie, at least, to be attacked by Ethiopians on the street. He breathed a sigh of relief when they escaped incident.

Negussie said little about the dangers he'd survived, but by visiting Addis, John was getting a clearer picture of the violence Ethiopians risked walking into, day by day. John was shaken. He was thankful for Negussie's evident protection, but he knew Christians were facing increasing persecution. John couldn't help feeling uneasy about his friend's future.

Their final parting was one of the most poignant leave-takings of John's life. The two stood at the Press gate trying to swallow the lumps in their throats, like Jonathan and David of old. They embraced in the formal Ethiopian way, shoulder to shoulder, touching one cheek to the other not once, but three times. Finally the brothers spontaneously held each other tight in one long bear hug. John kept looking back as he walked up the hill to his parents' house after Negussie had disappeared through the gate. *When will we meet again?*

The rainy season seemed to weep with them that day.

FACING MARXISM

Negussie looked over the dull brown fields around Wolisso with a sense of being back where he had started. In January, Ethiopia's lushness fades as ever-more-bony cattle scrounge to find fodder. The harvest is over and the long months of dryness take their toll. Prayer goes up for the "small rains" due in March to be adequate to avert the yearly possibility of drought.

By March 1977, Negussie had finished his training, had taught in Addis a while, and then had taken a teaching position in his home area in Wolisso. He missed Ato Tekle's fatherly leadership. By now, his former principal had been elected as the national church's first General Secretary, so he too had migrated to Addis. Ato Tekle was serving the church born out of SIM, called the *Kale Heywet* Church (KHC), meaning "Word of Life." He was sleeping temporarily at headquarters in a small office over the mission chapel and traveling home to see his family when he could. With the growing anti-religion rhetoric of the government, pressures upon national church leaders were enormous.

Even teachers in down-country schools were affected by the atmosphere of fear. A bit misshapen though he was, Negussie was a vibrant witness to Christ, making him a dangerous person in the estimation of local political leadership. Although he realized the axe might fall, he continued to live normally, forthright about his faith. Like the three Ethiopian sergeants in Eritrea, he had resolved to be a Christian wherever he was.

He considered it a gift from God that he was posted for a time at a place near his father's alternate home. It was only an hour from Lake Bishoftu, where national Christians were beginning to gather secretly at the mission's guest facility. Tension was running high in educated young people, for they were the most vulnerable segment of the population. Arrest or conscription lurked in the background of their days and nights. When John Coleman mentioned in a letter that his college roommate was gone, leaving an empty bed, Negussie joked obliquely in his answer:

> John! Your Nuge really would like to sleep in the extra bed you have in your room. Well, I'm sure by this time your friend will be back and you won't have an extra bed. Otherwise I would have come to stay with you!

Young Christians were on the move in those days. A safe bed with a friend was not taken for granted.

Fear was Ethiopia's overwhelming emotion in 1977. For some, it became sheer terror. At the lowest level, young people were chosen by Party leaders as *cadres* to enforce communist doctrines in the local *kebele,* the neighborhood political association. Kebele leaders numbered every house and required every individual to register for his or her personal identification number, in order to be issued a passbook. The ID book would be demanded at barricaded checkpoints on travel routes, or upon arrest. Fear was fanned in various ways — by the watching cadre who demanded loyalty to the Revolution, by the sudden action of the local kebele taken against an individual without right of appeal, and by high-handed Party leaders skilled in intimidation. Such leaders might be committed to "the cause," or on the other hand they might just be pursuing personal interests or settling old scores under the cloak of Marxist "purity."

Either way, the populace learned to stay quiet about personal opinions and not to be seen if possible. Negussie's December 1977 letter made the oblique statement:

> I'm playing the guitar for the church...There are not as many people in church as before, but many blessings and comfort and full confidence in the Lord. No pressure from outside to take a man or woman from the Lord, but great pressures in individual lives have come to decision — to stay or go.

The intensification of fear in 1977 became known as the Red Terror. In the capital, shots rang out in the night. In the morning bodies were found propped up on street intersections, marked with warning signs designed to terrify the populace as they passed by on the way to work or school. "Look what happens to those who undermine the course of the Revolution!" Although the capital was home base to the process, the Red Terror was felt throughout the country by students and peasants, by poor people and rich. Each would later remember — or try to forget — his or her own experiences of that year.

A certain contemporary of Negussie's traveled from his home in Jimma through Wolisso to go to school in the capital. This fellow's experience shows what young people were up against. Lual (pseudonym) was one of six sons of a father who had become rich through owning several flourmills and a fleet of buses. Lual's family was nominally Orthodox. Highly idealistic, he went off to the university and found there in the incendiary talk of communist cadres a hope that the world's problems might be answered by "the rich sharing with the poor."

Lual's growing zeal for Marxism prompted Party leaders to appoint him to lead a team of *zemecha* (national service) campaigners to the south. His assignment was to target Pente-type Christians, to terrorize them, and to shut down their churches. His technique was to take up a position in a church building early Sunday morning along with other cadres on his team, and start haranguing the congregation, declaring loudly that religion had no part to play in the new Ethiopia. The cadres ridiculed people for "praying to an invisible god" as they attempted to empty the church.

One morning a simple peasant woman stood up in a beleaguered congregation and said, "In spite of all that you have told us, we came here to pray to God and we're going to pray before we leave." Before anyone could stop her, she led in prayer. The campaigners were furious and hustled her off to the local police station. They charged the praying woman with "resisting the Revolution."

She withstood their abuse quietly, unmoved. When she was released, her first act was to invite her accusers to her home for a meal. Arrogant as the cadres were, homecooked food sounded irresistible. Walking into her home, they salivated at the aroma of red peppers and savory spices in the *wut* dishes she had prepared. On the *mesob* (basket-woven low table) was spread a lovely *injera* pancake, piled with various meat and vegetable sauces, much like the fare their mothers made. Before inviting them to partake, their hostess went ahead and thanked God for the food, ignoring their forced laughter designed to drown her out.

The campaigners worked in that area for many weeks, trying to negate the influence of this humble peasant woman. However, neither their threats of imprisonment nor their weekly tirades in the churches succeeded in dispersing her or the other believers. When the cadres were finally scheduled to depart, a local political leader had to be chosen by kebele vote. Who was elected but their thorn in the flesh, the praying woman herself!

Back at the university again, Lual relentlessly continued to make life intolerable for believers there. In the cafeteria one day, he saw someone bow his head in prayer before eating. Lual jumped up and screamed at him, "Why are you thanking a non-existent deity for food that you bought yourself?" Then he struck the student a hard blow across the head.

Suddenly Lual felt his body go numb. *Why did I do that?* he asked himself. *The man had done nothing to me, and yet I hit him.* He recalled only a blur after that, as he stumbled about, not eating, not sleeping for days. The strongest memory was the reappearing face of the praying woman, full of love, who remained unbent after all his efforts to break her. Finally he stumbled into a church one morning. With his head covered under his white *gabi,* he cried out to God for mercy. Although he knew nothing about the Bible, he later dated his conversion to that moment. God promptly brought forth some believers to encourage him. They began to nurture him in a secret Bible study, hardly realizing that this modern-day "Saul" could become a "Paul."

Soon the young convert faced persecution of the most deadly sort from his own brother, now a colonel in the army. His brother invited him to a bar and ordered a beer for them both. When Lual asked for something different, his brother growled, "So it's true you've become a Christian!" Lual sensed danger and rose to leave, but then his brother reached for his revolver. "An enemy of the regime" could be killed without fear of legal reprisal. The younger brother raced from the bar, hotly pursued, praying for protection. He dashed through traffic, crossed the road, and found himself blocked by a high wall. A supernatural power helped him somehow scale the barrier and jump to safety on the other side.

The way the fugitive disguised himself and escaped out of Addis, how he got onto a bus going southward, by what means he slipped across the patrolled Ethiopian border to Kenya and made it on, penniless, to Nairobi, is a story of one divine deliverance after another, each episode strengthening his trust in God.

Eventually Lual found himself scrounging out life with rough-living refugees in the Kenyan capital. A surprising sequence occurred. Back home he had earlier disdained the Christian radio programs of the Radio Voice of the Gospel, a highly valued public service to Ethiopia provided by the Lutherans. In

1977, the Marxists confiscated RVOG and renamed it the "Revolutionary Voice of Ethiopia." Ousted missionaries had gone to Nairobi, where they began preparing programs in Amharic to beam into Ethiopia from the Seychelles islands off the coast of East Africa. Miraculously, while Lual was praying for leading in Nairobi, the exiled radio staff happened upon him. They asked if he would consider reading scripts in Amharic for radio broadcasts. Lual was taking a risk by exposing his voice to identification, but in God's mysterious providence, "Paul's" voice became an instructor and comforter to Ethiopian Christians whom "Saul" had formerly sought to persecute.

Those years of the Red Terror, 1977 and 1978, precipitated the departure of most foreigners from Ethiopia, although the Colemans did not leave until 1980. Missionary Aviation Fellowship kept running into riots that cadres staged when the pilots landed at various missions' far-flung airstrips in the south. Tipped off that their planes were about to be confiscated, MAF reluctantly decided to leave Ethiopia. Their departure would vastly affect the viability of remote mission stations in the bush. During their last two weeks of operation, MAF offered each remote station a single opportunity for air evacuation. The expatriate staff people of dozens of isolated stations made sudden, heart-wrenching departures. Furthermore, hundreds of mission schools, scores of clinics, and a number of hospitals were confiscated by the Marxist government. Mission personnel found themselves confined to the capital with nearly all places of service denied them.

Although mission leaders had hastily prepared the churches for this eventuality, the sudden exodus of these long-time spiritual mentors came as a shock to national constituencies. It left them floundering in unknown waters. Some turned bitter and vindictive, feeling abandoned. Nevertheless, God was faithful. He raised up leaders within the church to strengthen her people, men like Pastor Kaydamo in Addis. Such men helped downcountry believers as well, through specially called consultations.

They sometimes used the SIM's conference center an hour's drive south of Addis, the place Negussie knew well, called *Bishoftu*. The property was nestled along the shore of a lake named *Bobagaya* in the Oromo language. An extinct volcanic cone cradled this lovely lake rimmed by verdant trees and wildlife. The place was a near paradise, except for overhead maneuvers of planes coming in and out of the Ethiopian Air Base at the nearby town of Debre Zeit. Bishoftu had long been used for conferences and vacations by almost every mission in the country. Humanly speaking, it made no sense that this gem was not confiscated, but it seemed to experience angelic protection. In God's providence, this spot became strategically important to Ethiopian Christians during the Revolution as a secluded hideaway where believers could recharge their batteries.

By now, the three airmen from Shoa who Negussie had met in Asmara had been transferred back to the Debre Zeit Air Base. Eager to see people reached in their area, they sought the support of the Fellowship Church near the University in Addis. Down by Bishoftu lake a lovely little grass-roofed cottage enclosed in overhanging trees witnessed many a clandestine gathering such as baptismal services, the Lord's Supper, and special consultations. A group of nine Ethiopians — the three airmen and six others — had met in that little grass cottage one day, and the fellowship born out of that beginning was eventually to take root and become a large church of amazing vitality.

Although Girma and Solomon got out of the service, Teshome continued to fly to Asmara for two-week missions, doing maintenance on Ethiopian Air Force planes. When there, he quietly labored to strengthen believers at that base. Back in Debre Zeit, the threesome helped their flock withstand Marxist harassment — church closings, school confiscations, house stonings, and the like.

In these threatening days of what seemed like expatriate desertion, national leaders organized a conference at Bishoftu which was later remembered as "the crown conference." Among the speakers was an Ato Solomon, who had been an announcer for the Lutheran radio station. He spoke powerfully, for he was gifted as an apologist, had read widely, and could help people understand the claims of Marxism in juxtaposition with the truths of God. He never mentioned Marxism, but simply used the Old Testament as a text.

That conference would long be remembered for its powerful theme: "Hold onto your crown!" — an admonition from Christ's messages to the seven churches in Revelation. "Be faithful even to the point of death, and I will give you the crown of life," promised the Messiah who would finally reign. Key men like Solomon and Kaydamo were laboring diligently for God's glory, that their generation of believers would maintain firm confidence in their Lord. His was the admonition: "I am coming soon. Hold on to what you have, so that no one will take your crown."

As it happened, realizing that the future leadership of the church stood in grave danger, the national and mission leadership decided to try to get a few young leaders out of the country for a time. One sent abroad was Negussie's brilliant relative from Wolisso school days.

The national church was losing more and more of its supporting cast. The handful of Western missionaries that were left in the country knew little about life under communism firsthand. They could speak from research, although not from personal experience. They provided valuable materials, like Wurmbrand's "Tortured for Christ," from Romania, which was put into Amharic. Some of the expatriates who had done this kind of teaching, like Howard Brant, were forced out of the country. Furthermore, Ethiopians caught listening to a Westerner could be stoutly accused. *Who could come over and help us?* the Ethiopians wondered.

A CHINESE CONNECTION

Apparently the Ethiopians' "Macedonian call" (a watershed in the Apostle Paul's experience) was heard by a certain Chinese couple thousands of miles away. Yu Kwong Hseuh and his wife, Lily, had been doing a refresher course at All Nations Christian College in England, where they had met students from Africa who drew their attention to the Ethiopian situation. Yu Kwong was not new to the persecution of Christians, for after serving in the Sino-Japanese war (1937-1945), he had graduated from Nanking University and had to flee China in 1950, when he was about thirty. He and his wife taught in theological institutions in Hong Kong, Taiwan, Malaysia, and the Philippines. Meanwhile they kept in touch with Christians on the mainland, some of whom were imprisoned. Yu Kwong Hseuh had a close tie with the persecuted church, for he had been deeply touched by the life and writings of Wang Ming-Tau, who did not register his group in the Three Self Movement as demanded by the Chinese communist government. From the outside, Pastor Hsueh served the underground church by translating two of A.W. Tozer's books into Chinese, *Knowledge of the Holy* and *The Pursuit of God,* the latter of which was printed twelve times in Hong Kong.

The Hsuehs had been praying about Ethiopia while they were in England. A surprise gift from a Christian couple in the United States made the trip financially possible. Someone wrote to Paul Balisky, the new head of GBI, on behalf of Yu Kwong, introducing him as a Chinese Christian. Upon arrival of the tall Chinese pastor, Mr. Balisky canceled GBI classes for three days to allow their guest all the time possible with students.

Every sinew of Paul Balisky's wiry frame bent to hear the first message. Being himself a Canadian whose family had emigrated from the Ukraine, Paul had some background related to repression. *What will this man center upon?* Paul wondered, as he studied this dignified Chinese Christian. Pastor Hsueh's focus during that first visit came from a passage in John 19, in which John was the only Apostle who stayed close during the Lord's crucifixion. "Who will do the same, in Ethiopia? The time has come that if you want to be faithful to God," he said, "you must pay the price."

Back in Addis, Mr. Balisky and the Colemans arranged discreet ways for Yu Kwong to meet with a broad range of Christian groups. When his departure time drew near, they expressed their hope to him: "Your work here is not finished. You must come again!" Actually, that became the first of six trips Pastor Hseuh made to Ethiopia.

Back in England, Pastor Hsueh told his wife that they were invited for the next year. Tiny but strong, Lily's supportive presence and excellent English enhanced their ministry on the second trip. At Jimma, the atmosphere was charged, for the school was threatened with imminent closure. Students asked very sensitive questions, questions missionaries couldn't answer.

Obedience, Yu Kwong said, was the key issue. Fear was everywhere, for people were being arrested, or just disappeared. Yu Kwong's answer was simply stated: "Fear God, fear no man."

For six weeks the Hseuhs traveled down country for secret meetings with Christians in four provinces. Paul Balisky and Murray Coleman were amused at some checkpoints, where they heard onlooking cadres whisper, "This Chinaman must be from the Derg. Pass him through!" Chinese communists were moving in large numbers throughout Ethiopia in those days.

In Addis, in one period of two days, the Hsuehs spoke to nine groups. During that visit, Yu Kwong challenged people with God's admonition in Isaiah 41: "Do not fear, for I am with you; do not be dismayed, for I am your God. I will strengthen you and help you; I will uphold you with my righteous right hand. All who rage against you will surely be ashamed and disgraced..." Chinese believers had taken God at His word and could testify that they had found themselves upheld.

At one meeting, a dozen Ethiopian young people present had already been in prison, sometimes repeatedly. Their Chinese brother's response was warm and straightforward: "It is worthy to suffer for Christ. God is with you. Remain faithful. Carry on." Sometimes Yu Kwong encouraged Ethiopians in their hour of testing with testimonies from China's struggle with persecution. His friend Wang Ming-Tau was incarcerated for twenty-three years. Watchman Nee, known in America for his book *The Normal Christian Life,* was to be released after fifteen years, but when he would not write a "repentance" document, he was kept in prison until he died.

"We felt the presence of the Holy Spirit at every meeting," Pastor Hsueh reiterated later. "Repeatedly we saw fruit from the previous visit. One man told us, 'I wasn't a believer when you came last year and preached from John, but now I am.' Another man said, 'I practically memorized all the points of Yu Kwong's message last year,' as he introduced me at a meeting the second year. The first year, a Marxist police chief came, thinking there would be no hope for him. I didn't talk to him personally, but the next year he appeared and was himself the interpreter as I spoke from the book of Daniel."

And so it was that God provided shepherds for Ethiopian believers. Through the Hsuehs and other Christians well acquainted with life under communism, Ethiopians were encouraged in their desperate hour. They discovered their oneness in the Body of Christ and heard how God had transformed other people's worst experiences into fruitfulness.   Principles for living under atheistic control were passed around among believers in underground house meetings.   The Ethiopian church, like others around the world, learned to develop strategies for survival.   In the end, survival did not turn out to be the only result.   The believers were being purified and strengthened so powerfully that countless people were irresistibly drawn into the dynamic fellowship of this persecuted but victorious remnant so alive with God's presence.

One of these believers was a young woman named Fantaye, who soon would become deeply important to Negussie.

MAGNET OF
THE HEART

Fantaye had grown up a city girl. Now a high school graduate, well educated for Ethiopia, she wondered what life would bring her. Over her family's home, planes from Addis Ababa International Airport grazed the sky. Hers had been a city schooling in a metropolitan hub with skyscrapers, factories, and stately boulevards that hosted the offices of the Organization of African Unity and nearly a hundred embassies. Now Marxism had arrived en masse, flooding the city with Russians, Cubans, and Chinese. She wondered what these new *ferenge* (foreigners) would bring.

Fantaye's relatives were Orthodox Christians, as were the majority of Ethiopians in Addis. More than forty Ethiopian Orthodox churches dotted the city. Over two hundred feasts or fasts were sprinkled over the Ethiopian calendar. At high church holidays in her youth, Fantaye and her brothers thrilled with anticipation as holiday foods were prepared and a parade day drew near. They donned their best clothes. Fantaye was a well-built, attractive girl with a strong face and gentle eyes. She looked stunning in her white *kamis* and *shashe* (dress and head shawl) worn on holiday occasions, her hems decorated with a rich bright border edged in gold, and an Orthodox cross embroidered in matching colors, across her chest. At the holiday called *Meskel* ("cross") celebrating "the finding of the true cross," they could hardly wait for the evening bonfires to be set in neighborhood squares all over town. At *Genna* (Christmas) on January 7th, the church services and home feasting were wonderful. Late in January *Timkat* ("baptism") came, the most exciting holiday of all, a three-day celebration of Christ's baptism, featuring the reconfirmation of the Orthodox community. The whole city lined the streets as each church's *Tabot* (Ark) was taken from its enclosure in the sanctuary's Holy of Holies and paraded to the Jan Meda race grounds. Priests would "dance before the Lord," as in David's time, while the processions moved down the streets. Each velvet-draped Ark was surrounded by turbaned priests wearing colorful capes and carrying brightly sequined umbrellas and forked prayer sticks. In the open field, the draped and guarded Arks would spend the night amid thousands of priests and celebrants. Spotted over the scene, people sold food and religious trinkets and riders raced horses festooned in red. What more could a child ask?

But now the responsibilities of adulthood were beginning to loom larger on Fantaye's horizon. Someday she would be the mother to prepare the feast. That was a woman's role. But new roles seemed to be appearing, now that Marxism had come. Holidays were muted now. While the Orthodox churches were not closed, their domain was seriously cut back by the Revolution. The church had held its biggest celebrations at Meskel Square, named for Jesus' cross. It was renamed "Red Square" now. The populace had to appear at Party demonstrations there, or else risk fines or imprisonment. Women going out on *zemecha* were encouraged to carouse with men, and women were even going to war. She pondered the society around her, wondering, *Where do I fit in all this?*

Fantaye's gnawing hunger for what was true and good in life had led her to search farther than most young women of her acquaintance. Long hours standing at attention in the church yard while religious services were conducted in Orthodoxy's holy language, Ge'ez, left her wondering what the priests' unintelligible words really meant. A friend had told her that one could learn wonderful things out of the Holy Bible from teaching offered in Amharic on the Addis radio station, RVOG.

Alone in her room, Fantaye listened time after time to talk about Jesus across the airwaves. She became convinced of the Lord Jesus Christ's supremacy above all others, not only as the "one mediator between God and man," but as the one who had given His life to cancel out the death penalty she knew her own sinfulness warranted. Believing this testimony from the Scriptures, she received Jesus as "the Word-become-flesh." Was he not alive from the dead, the Messiah Himself? Did He not bid her to come to Him for her every need?

The radio messages of RVOG fed her soul. What a loss it was to her, and to countless others, when the Marxists swept into the radio station one day and destroyed the teaching tapes of this one rival doctrine they most feared.

Like many others, Fantaye began to quietly make her way to underground meetings to seek spiritual sustenance. In a home where she gathered with other believers one night in 1978, an out-of-town visitor from Wolisso slipped in. It was a night neither he nor she could forget. Negussie's focus was pulled like a magnet toward the young woman across the room. She was among others he had met in the home that night. Why did she stand out to him so? She was of average height, with a strong face. Was it her kind smile, or almost liquid eyes? He'd been to underground meetings in Addis before. Guarded as they had to be, they were wonderful times of worship, study and corporate encouragement in the difficult circumstances all were facing. Why should this one person stand out from the group, rising in his mind's eye after the meeting, continuing with him as he made the trip back to Wolisso, visiting his thoughts when the school day closed and he was trying to prepare for the next day's teaching? What did it mean, her strange lingering with him, so unfamiliar a presence in his bachelorhood?

In his late twenties by now, Negussie had maintained his singleness carefully, bent upon pleasing his Lord in all aspects of his life. What was God's purpose for this meeting? *Could she ever be drawn to one such as myself? Might our paths cross again?*

They did, very briefly, on his next trip to Addis. There she was again across the room, so graceful and composed. Together they shared the experience of the group, his heart singing while his fingers strummed the guitar he loved to play, happy simply to be worshiping together with her through song.

Would she correspond with him? he quietly asked afterward. She would, she replied.

And Fantaye? She went home and pondered too. Only a month before their first meeting, she had specifically asked the Lord to bring to her a godly husband. She was only twenty-one. Her prayer was looking into the future, eager to commit this crucial area of her life to Him. Already, she was experiencing loneliness in a home that did not appreciate her singular devotion to the Lord Jesus Christ.

Her Amhara family practiced Orthodoxy by keeping the festivals, fasts, and feasts prescribed by the church calendar — hundreds each year. Specific days were given to a myriad of biblical personages and angels and martyrs, along with members of the Trinity. The Virgin Mary seemed to be the most venerated of all; her intercessions were considered the most efficacious. Fantaye had often stood with the women outside the church, if during her menstruation, or sometimes inside the vestibule, where priests chanted the ancient prayers in Ge'ez. Only recently, since listening to RVOG, had she begun to experience God in a personal way. Now she could not hear enough about Him.

Fantaye had gone home from the evening of Negussie's first appearance strangely stirred. She rehearsed her reactions. Across the room she had seen the visitor from Wolisso, an unusually short man. Her eyes wandered over the group, but kept moving back to his countenance. He radiated such unusual joy. Standing not taller than herself, his form, she had to admit, "did not please my eyes." Yet she did not despise him. She wondered what had stunted his torso, for his legs were long and his face seemed deeply mature. The man so reflected the inner presence of the One she'd come to love, that she was instinctively drawn to him.

Thus began the keeping of her long secret, not voiced to others, or even to Negussie, for a long time. Yet as they met periodically, her warm eyes spoke volumes, stirring hope within him. Now Negussie made periodic trips to the little one-room post office in Wolisso town, looking for a letter from Fantaye in addition to his correspondence with John in Canada.

One never knew in these days when a message would bear good or tragic news. One day word of his teenage comrade, Tesfaye, reached Negussie. His last clue about Tesfaye's whereabouts was hearing that he'd been stationed with the Ethiopian army in Asmara. Negussie's pilgrimage and Tesfaye's had both shared life in Asmara, but they'd passed like ships in the night, a few months apart. "Tesfaye was killed in the battle for Massawa," the brief report said. Death on the battlefield was striking down the choicest of Ethiopia's youth, and Eritrea's too. Negussie wept.

The civil war and the Revolution continued to impact everyone's personal life. Fantaye had taken her place in the workforce as an accountant with the Ministry of Health. But crossing the city to get to work could be a terrible experience. Bloodied bodies lay on the streets in the early hours, horrifying bypassers. Unexpected roadblocks and credential inspections were frightening. Suspicious employees in the office who threatened to incriminate co-workers made work tense. At night, the media put out a steady stream of Marxist propaganda in jargon unfamiliar to Ethiopian ears. The papers reported political executions and casualties on the battlefields of the Eritrean or Somali warfronts. The Marxist government's grand inauguration of "the Cultural Revolution," meant that "the broad masses" were expected to parade long hours at Revolution Square.

None of these sensitive issues were safe for the letters Fantaye sent to Negussie, which might be censored. But they were not central to their developing friendship anyway. Sharing their relationship with the Lord was the central focus of their correspondence. Her letters came as priceless treasures to be read and reread, lighting up his world, a world now darkened by the militant indoctrination that teachers were all ordered to attend weekly.

Negussie's experience had already broadened his perspective. He'd seen what was happening in the north, and was regularly exposed to the situation in the capital. He knew that GBI had finally been forcibly closed, scattering the students and landing Paul and Lila Balisky in Addis. His own area was experiencing intensified communist pressure, too. He knew that the basic tenets of dialectical materialism cut across his deep commitment to God. He had to go to the teachers' weekly indoctrination meetings, enduring them along with an earnest friend named Mulugeta.

Christians could either avoid trouble by acquiescing publicly, or else risk suspicion and probable mistreatment if they did not hide their witness for Christ. Negussie complied with regulations as far as he felt he could, but decided not to compromise his faith into silence. He would share discreetly with any people God sent to him. He led a small Bible study for those who showed interest, and shared the Scriptures with those who appeared hungry to listen. He was careful not to flaunt his convictions in the classroom, but his life spoke unmistakably of an assurance and peace which was not appreciated by local cadres, some of whom were former classmates. When he was promoted, it put him in an even more enviable position. Negussie was popular, for students sensed his impartial attitudes and genuine interest in them. When those with sincere questions came to visit him in the evenings, he talked openly with them about the claims of the Lord Jesus Christ.

Cadres watched for a chance to incriminate or get rid of him. Negussie couldn't help suspecting that a trap was being laid for him and he wondered, *When will it snap shut?*

A method emerged. How better to punish him than by putting him away in some backwater village? On his next visit to Addis, Negussie broke the news to Fantaye that he'd been moved to a little school in the Gindo area northwest of Wolisso, where he knew no one. The demotion and isolation were hard to take for one so well trained and gregarious. Even there, kebele leaders watched him with cool calculation, noting who visited him at night. In the lonely hours, he wrote to Fantaye or to John. Chris Ott, the German nurse who awarded him his first Bible, received a letter from Negussie during those lonely months. One line stood out: "I have chosen the way of the cross leading to glory." He seemed to sense what might be coming.

On their fourth meeting in Addis, Fantaye was delighted to supply Negussie with some Christian tracts, for he was always looking for ways to help people understand who Jesus could be to them. Most people hardly owned a book, and even a short pamphlet was valued. She hoped to hear the tracts were finding their way into receptive hands.

One night about that same time, she was caught in a raid on her underground meeting and was imprisoned along with others. So many buildings had been commandeered into jails that cadres couldn't hold people more than a few weeks, so they aimed at giving captives a horribly indelible lesson. These prison periods often left scars on body, mind, and soul — both on the victims and their captors.

When Fantaye got free, she rushed to the post office to get the letters that had come in her absence, but there were none. She wanted to let Negussie know why she hadn't written, so she wrote a letter that put the incident in code language, in case their mail was opened.

Strangely, still no response came. He'd been in Gindo six months now. She risked making a phone call to get information, but was told curtly, "Negussie is not here." Alarmed, she waited anxiously for some explanation. Others of her acquaintance had also simply dropped out of sight, never to return. *Oh my Lord Jesus,* she asked, *where is Negussie?*

THE TRAP
SNAPS SHUT

Negussie had been pleased with Fantaye's tracts and some
pocket New Testaments he had procured in Addis, for Christian
literature was in scarce supply. Back at Gindo a couple of searching students came by one night, had tea and listened to Negussie's
testimony and explanation of the good news. They eagerly took
two of the New Testaments. Soon after, a couple of teachers
came by. "Why don't you give us New Testaments like you did
to those two students?" they asked. Teachers were under pressure to turn in anyone that opposed or did not fully support the
Revolution. At the next Friday afternoon political rally, the two
stood and accused Negussie of "spreading a foreign religion."
Their initial charge? The "anti-revolutionary act of giving out
New Testaments."

Cadres hustled him off to a local jail, but not without rum-
maging through his belongings, which included John's and
Fantaye's letters. When he was transferred to the Wolisso police
station, those letters became the evidence of his supposed "CIA
connection," although John was from Canada, not the United
States. Fantaye's letters were their "evidence of an immoral relationship with a woman" — to heap character assassination
upon political accusation. His enemies added "Pente" to his
crimes. Although coined as a religious differentiation before
the Revolution, the term "Pente" by now had taken on political

flavor to insinuate that a person harbored "anti-revolutionary" attitudes.

The night of his arrest, his captors had to hustle their prey across a river, picking their way over a fallen tree. Negussie happened to be the only one present with a flashlight. He graciously escorted all of them across the fallen tree, one by one. There was also an older Orthodox priest among those who had accused him. Negussie escorted him and treated him with the great respect in which older people are held in Ethiopia. The next day the priest came to tell Negussie that he had misjudged him and that he apologized for his part in the arrest. Although the priest withdrew his accusations, the Marxist administrator of the Wolisso area decided to make a public example of Negussie, for he was known as a close friend of the former missionaries whose influence the new leadership wished to wipe out.

At the District offices, Negussie protested that he had no connections with foreign governments, but would confirm that he was a member of the Kingdom of God.

"If you simply renounce this foreign religion you can be released," he was told.

"I would rather die than deny my Lord," he flatly responded.

"Your choice," they jeered.

A police station was not a good place to be at the mercy of accusers. With former restraints now removed under Marxism, they became sites of uncontrolled mistreatment and torture. Inhuman experiments in brutality erupted, and women suffered unspeakably sometimes as well. Cadres exercised the upper hand in ways designed to break the will of a dissenter and to terrify those who heard his or her chilling screams from the outside. Red Terror deaths had given way to the black terror of torture, as if the depravity of man had been given *carte blanche*.

Negussie's interrogators took him to a room with two tables spanned by a pole. They prepared him for an often-used torture technique, tying his ankles together. Next they bound his wrists and bent him over to tie them to his ankles. The torture team offered him one last chance to recant. Then they stuffed a gag in his mouth and told him to raise a finger when he had had enough. "You just recant, and we stop!"

The pole was thrust under his bound hands and feet, and then lifted up to span the tables, leaving the victim hanging with head hanging down and bare feet exposed upwards. A soldier of rank began beating the soles of Negussie's feet with a heavy cane. When the man grew tired, he pulled out Negussie's gag and screamed, "Are you ready to recant?" By this time huge blood blisters had formed on the teacher's feet, but Negussie gasped out, "I'm ready to die for my Lord Jesus Christ."

An infuriated cadre started kicking his victim's head like a football. The man took hold of the ends of the ropes and strung them between Negussie's fingers and toes, pulling them tight to cut the flesh. He pulled out toenails. He picked up a club and lashed out at the feet again, bursting the blisters. Blood spurted all over Negussie's body. As the cadre beat on in a diabolical frenzy, the other men began to worry that the victim might die. They did not want to have to bury a corpse at night. Negussie's legs were swelling up like tree trunks, so the cadre finally stopped. The battered prisoner was nearly unconscious and unable to stand. They carried him over and dumped him on the prison floor.

As Negussie lay in his own blood, he was a picture of his Savior's own suffering. He could have called out like Christ, "My God, my God, why have you forsaken me?" Psalm 22, which he knew well, went on to describe his own state:

> ...I am a worm and not a man, scorned by men and despised by the people. All who see me mock me; they hurl insults, shaking their heads: 'He trusts in the LORD; let the LORD rescue him. Let him deliver him, since he delights in him.' ...Do not be far

from me, for trouble is near and there is no one to help...I am poured out like water and all my bones are out of joint. My heart has turned to wax; it has melted away within me. My strength is dried up like a potsherd, and my tongue sticks to the roof of my mouth; you lay me in the dust of death. Dogs have surrounded me; a band of evil men has encircled me, they have pierced my hands and my feet...

As he focused upon the Savior, Negussie's soul and body stirred with returning life. For many weeks, he was unable to walk. He was obliged to depend upon other prisoners to carry him even to the toilet, a filthy area where they dumped him. Negussie faced unspeakable suffering. A friend on the outside who caught sight of him through a fence could hardly recognize him, except for the telling mark of his hunched back.

However, Negussie testified that he was miraculously shielded from pain during the initial torture. "I thought I was dead, but the Lord wanted me to live," he affirmed later. Willingness to be struck down and even die was a decision he had already made. Had not his Lord stated a principle of the Kingdom: "Except a corn of wheat fall into the ground and die, it abideth alone"? Somehow, already "counting himself dead" freed Negussie to live without further fear of death.

Eventually he was able to slip out a message with someone going to Addis, telling Fantaye where he was. Of course, he had not discovered that she, too, had been imprisoned. She was relieved to find out where he was, but cringed to learn of his dangerous location.

As soon as she could arrange it, she made a secret trip to Wolisso, carrying a little parcel of fruit as a gift. At the jail, they refused to allow her to see him, but did not deny his presence there. She wept bitterly and begged the guards, "He's my brother. I cannot go without seeing him!" Fantaye did not feel she lied when she begged to see her "brother." Was he not a brother to her through the family of believers and their deepening friendship in Christ? The authorities finally agreed to allow her five minutes with the prisoner.

Negussie could hardly believe his eyes and wept for joy that she had come. "Be prepared, they want to question you," he whispered, before they were torn apart. Few words could be exchanged, and what she learned of his suffering was pieced together later. Heartbroken at his battered appearance and helpless to aid his release, she stumbled out and quickly made her way back to Addis. There she knew no one to whom she felt she could turn. She could only pour out her heart to her closest Friend, and wait.

The next months were a nightmare of mistreatment for Negussie. Long years later, the marks of torture remained visible on his body. Local friends grieved over his condition. The teacher who had gone through the local brainwashing sessions with Negussie, Mulugeta, had a great affection for him. He ached over the beatings his friend took and asked the brotherhood to uphold him in prayer. Looking back later, Mulugeta compared the effect of Negussie's imprisonment to Paul's. "His testimony strengthened people on the outside. Even though he seemed weak in body, they gave him no sympathy. Even for a healthy person it was hard, and so it seemed to me impossible for him to shoulder it. But by God's grace, he did. The faith!"

That very summer of 1979, John Coleman again made his way to Ethiopia to visit his family. He was burned out from college, and as it happened, he stayed on a year. John was yearning to see his old friend.

When he arrived and found that Negussie was imprisoned, he was cut to the heart. He wondered if he might visit him. Yet, for an "imperialist" foreigner to show interest in Negussie would only increase hostility against him. So by way of Negussie's sister who lived in Addis, the Colemans sent a little gift to him. It was a strange one, a bug repellent called "Soap and Flit," a boon to prisoners confined to infested quarters.

Negussie managed to send back a package to the Colemans through Ato Tekle, who made a visit to Negussie's cell. Although Tekle went there planning to encourage a downcast man, the prisoner actually did most of the encouraging. Negussie handed his weary old friend a little money he had saved from selling handwork. It was to help suffering believers on the outside, he said. "Tell them to keep the faith!"

Together the Colemans opened the package Tekle delivered to them. Inside were decorated ball point pens for each of the family with designs Negussie had woven around the cartridges with scraps of various-colored thread. And there was a special gift for John, a white, brimmed hat that Negussie had knit with hairpins.

Enclosed was a card that looked like directions, titled "Six steps for washing, drying, blocking, and stretching the hat" but it included a hidden message. It read:

> To My Dear Friend John and all my Family:
>
> Daily He gives me unspeakable joy and comfort. I am completely well and healthy. I have received the Soap and Flit you sent me. May God bless you. If God wills, I hope to see you after I receive the verdict. Acts 20:24, Phil. 1:20. I am sending this small gift to my dear brother John. I am your son Negussie Kumbi.

The Colemans looked up Negussie's code message, Paul's words in Acts and Philippians. The sentences spoke volumes:

Acts 20:24 read: "However, I consider my life worth nothing to me, if only I may finish the race and complete the task the Lord Jesus has given me — the task of testifying to the gospel of God's grace."

Phil. 1:20 said: "I eagerly expect and hope that I will in no way be ashamed, but will have sufficient courage so that now as always Christ will be exalted in my body, whether by life or by death."

FROM CAGE
TO CAGE

Fantaye's heart leapt when the news came: "Negussie has made an appeal and they've moved him to Addis!"

She had been carrying her burden in secret, speaking only to God about him. *He is right here in my own city!* she thought. *Women take food to their prisoners every day. Surely I could go sometimes too, even if secretly.*

With cadres trying out new forms of persuasion and due process of law evaporating, Negussie had decided that appealing his case to the central government might be the better part of wisdom. So it was that in January of 1979, he was moved to Addis and put in detention at an interrogation center which was located near the city's most sophisticated shopping area, the Piazza.

Although torture was employed less there, security was tighter. In fact, to go there to see him, Fantaye learned, would raise suspicion. After all, one of the charges against Negussie involved "letters from a woman" — a woman not identified as his wife, or sister, or mother. Not even a cousin.

The Ministry of Health had assigned Fantaye to work outside the city in the wider Shoa region. For a time Butajira was her post, a town halfway to Hosanna in a Muslim area. Ato Matewos who'd trained at SIM's Soddo Hospital had a pharmacy there. He was highly respected in the community, but when Marxist leadership took over, they sought to discredit him. They arrested a group of young people associated with Matewos one night and Fantaye narrowly escaped imprisonment. She had to hide out in someone's home until the coast was clear.

When she was able to travel back to her parents' home, she had occasion to shop in the Piazza. Going there was painful — to be in the midst of bustling crowds bent on business while her own heart was pulled like a magnet toward Negussie's prison. He'd warned her in Wolisso that she might be questioned. She was afraid of complicating his case now by trying to visit him. She could only stare longingly at the walls behind which he was caged.

When a summons for questioning was eventually delivered to her, she was frightened. As it turned out, the interrogators picked up no criminal evidence, and getting that ordeal over with actually proved helpful. It cleared the air for her and helped them narrow down the charges against Negussie to "suspicion of being CIA." Even that charge was unreasonable, for the letters from John Coleman were from Canada, not the United States.

Along with others at the detention center, Negussie's daily sufferings came from the very earthy experience of sharing a tiny room with little ventilation with a crush of unwashed human beings. On a regimented schedule, prisoners could be released from the stifling cell toward just one destination, the reeking toilet. Rats added their own form of terror at night.

Eventually, an intermediate verdict on the Wolisso man's case was reached. They moved him from the crowded interrogation center to Kerchaylee, a big prison down at Akaki in the southern part of Addis. It was there that the sixty-some ministers of the Emperor's government had been executed on the infamous Bloody Saturday.

The day of his transfer, Negussie looked up at the wide sky and thanked God! *Air...light...space...what luxuries!* Kerchaylee boasted an open prison yard. It was the dry season by then, and bright sunlight overhead could cheer prisoners as well as people who were free. Beware a south wind, however! A stench swept over the exercise yard when the wind came from the direction of the slaughterhouse area nearby. Attendant vultures circled above the general area, making the prisoners feel even more like prey.

When the word of Negussie's transfer came to Fantaye, her reactions were mixed. So many women took food there that she could slip in unnoticed, she felt. But Kerchaylee was known as a life-sentence prison. It was nicknamed Alem Buckagn, a wail of relinquishment meaning "life out in the world is over for me, ended." *Will it be so for him?*

Fantaye considered carefully how to at least get sight of Negussie. She knew his sister or someone from his family would deliver food to his new location, for Ethiopian prisoners got no food except what people brought to them. Fantaye decided a Sunday would be the best day to make her first attempt. She had to board several buses to make connections to the Kerchaylee prison gate that first Sunday morning. Her heart pounded in her rib cage with fear and anticipation. Trying to melt into the crowd of people carrying provisions, she hoped her little satchel of fruit helped her fit into the scene. No one yet knew of her connection with Negussie, not even his half-sister Alemaz, who might well be the one carrying Negussie's food supply that morning. Could she avoid being noticed? Fantaye could not claim to be a wife or family member. Would the authorities let her in?

She watched as people crowded up to a wire fence while prisoners looked longingly from the other side for someone who had come for their own sake. Fantaye spotted a familiar face in the crowd: sure enough, Alemaz. Fantaye stepped back out of sight. Watching where Alemaz moved to, she caught her first sight of Negussie since their few moments together in Wolisso. How privileged she felt just to be there.

She watched Alemaz soon depart out the gate, and then moved up into the front line to make herself noticeable. She raised up her little satchel of fruit. Negussie would never forget that first sight of Fantaye at Kerchaylee. She took his breath away. They met only momentarily as she handed the fruit over the fence, but more passed between them than an onlooker could ever know.

From that day on, the fondest expectation of Negussie's week would be those few moments when they could meet each other through eye and heart, perhaps speak a few words, and each be assured the other was well. Fantaye's family did not know just where she went each Sunday. After the prison stop, she attended an underground Bible study in a home, the low-key kind of fellowship in hushed tones that usually went unnoticed across the city. This became the pattern of her life for longer than she could have guessed. When they parted weekly at the fence, they both asked God for comfort. *At our age,* Fantaye thought, *this should be a time of beginning, and here we are meeting at "the end of the world."*

END OF THE
WORLD?

Negussie knew better than most what the "end" or "the world" really meant, so he paid little heed to his "Alem Buckagn" address. He set about cheering prison mates with whom he shared the compound. Some were incarcerated as criminals. Others were there as "politically accused." Here was a group of men badly in need of hope, and Negussie had abundant hope.

It was not that he had to talk much, for his attitude and countenance was so different from the norm that people were drawn to him instinctively, curious to figure out why he could still smile. They felt welcomed into Negussie's life, someone strangely free from obsession with his own situation. Many of them had given themselves to the Marxist cause, served it energetically, but had come out on the short end of the continuous jockeying for power. Being accused by another Marxist was a bitter pill to swallow. It led some even to death, just as they had dealt the same to others. What an ironic reversal to mull over in the long prison hours.

Negussie discovered other believers among the prisoners, and three of them purposely teamed up. Whenever they sensed a searching heart, they shared the tools for survival which were serving them well. The Epistle to the Ephesians had taught them what God had provided. Their "sword" was the word of God, their "shield" was faith. Negussie and his friends were testing out God's armory and, by experience, were proving his word to be their best offensive weapon, and faith in Him to be their mightiest defense.

Most cellmates were as imprisoned by self-absorption, anger, and despair as by locked gates. Furthermore, each knew he might have to face "the final solution." No one knew who would be executed, or when. With death hanging over them, prisoners of Alem Buckagn had to consider whether the Marxists were right, that life ends in the grave, or might there be life after death, as the ancient church had affirmed? During miserable nights, haunting questions would torment them: *When I am shot, will I be extinct... or judged? What will my destination be — a senseless body eaten by worms underground, as dialectical materialism teaches? Or might I find myself in heaven...or in hell?*

Throughout his years in prison, Negussie walked through the valley of the shadow with some who were never released. He talked repeatedly with a certain man who stoutly refused to receive the message that Negussie so earnestly shared. "No," he kept insisting, "no!" But the man had no peace. He surveyed his own despairing condition, in such contrast to the hope that Negussie's life authenticated.

Finally, he made the choice to put his trust in the saving work of the Lord Jesus, the Christ. A great change began to come over this prisoner. Life took on a fullness he could not have believed could be his in such circumstances. Still, the hour of his summons finally came. He went to his new Christian brothers and broke the news. "I am to be executed. Yet, amazingly, I have peace, for I know where I am going." He embraced them, expecting to meet again, and took his place before the firing squad.

New prisoners replaced those who were gone. Among those who turned up at Kerchaylee was a very young fellow from way down in Gamo Gofa. Tadesse was not much taller than Negussie. He'd been arrested on the streets of Addis for distributing Christian literature. This was not Tadesse's first incarceration, for the fellow seemed to survive one close call after another, by God's grace. Christians in his isolated southwestern province had suffered more persecution and imprisonment than most places, probably because of a Muslim provincial governor named Ali Musa. The man was infamous for brutality. He'd had people buried alive at Shashamane, where Negussie had visited the Colemans. The Shashamane Leprosarium's director, Dr. Mulatu, had barely escaped mob execution there.

Tadesse had come into an experience of faith in the Lord Jesus very early in his youth, and quickly affected people around him. His testimony in the countryside and in marketplaces had resulted in hundreds of people turning from animism to Christ. He taught and organized youth in the area, challenging them to share the powerful news of Christ with others.

A slight young lad only around fifteen, Tadesse irritated the Marxists. How could this runt of a youth have such influence on the very young people they were assigned to enlist for their Revolutionary cause? Tadesse kept turning up telling any local people who would listen to him about the living Jesus, to whom he testified convincingly. Infuriated, they accused him: "You are brainwashing our youth with your idealistic teaching!" Cadres repeatedly disciplined him, and one final encounter looked as if it would be his last. Negussie and his Alem Buckagn friends listened as Tadesse reenacted his experience.

The town was Arba Minch, where Lake Chamo and Abaya almost converge. Up on Chencha Mountain above the lakes, lived a strong community of Christians. Ato Tesfaye, who'd been another older married student when Ato Tekle was at GBI, led them. As it turned out, Tesfaye and his elders would soon go to prison themselves. But down the mountain, the belligerent young cadres engineered showdowns in their city headquarters.

It was heady stuff for young cadres to wield power over people, and it was not surprising that they often developed that brash arrogance and enjoyment of power to which human nature is prone. This particular group hustled Tadesse off and worked him over with a routine form of torture, beating the soles of his feet with iron rods. The pain was excruciating and the injury was increased afterward by making the victim walk over thistles or thorns. Expecting this lesson to be a conclusive, the cadres turned him loose but gave Tadesse a formal order: "Leave this Christianity, join us, and close your 'church work.' Be still from now on about this 'good news of Jesus' or else take the consequences."

When he could walk again, he was caught testifying and another showdown ensued. Ten of them took the slight figure to a storage hall that day, stripped him and ordered him to lie prostrate on the floor between a row of five cadres on each side. In turn they beat his naked body with rawhide whips. They were sure that this disciplinary action would make the rebel think hard before spreading any more of what they saw as counter-revolutionary teaching. Since these cadres had been brought in from other areas, they could not have known what an unusual youth they were dealing with.

Shortly after the lashing torture, Tadesse again was caught encouraging people to give themselves to the Lord Jesus Christ. Again he was dragged into jail and made to strip and prepare for another beating.

"Now... what is your intention?" they challenged. "Tell us what you plan to do!" "My ... aim?" Tadesse answered slowly. "As long as I am alive, my aim is to learn God's word and to teach it. If someone stops me, I will die for this."

The group stood there, discomfited. They argued among themselves, and eventually released the unbending Tadesse. Their threats only strengthened his resolve to continue testifying.

Of course he was arrested again. They must silence this irredeemable counter-revolutionary once and for all, they reasoned. "We're not going to beat you this time," they announced to him. "This time we're going to kill you. This will be your last day." As he awaited their action, Tadesse managed to slip out a note that revealed his situation and begged urgently for prayer. Someone rushed the note up to the elders who were meeting that very day on Chencha Mountain, a meeting to which Tadesse had been called. The gospel had first reached these Chencha people only thirty years before.

Late that afternoon about twenty determined cadres walked their prisoner to the windowless storage hall to settle the matter. Tadesse stood in the midst of the angry group who were nearly all taller and older than their prey. The little dimple that sometimes appeared on one side of his lips trembled slightly. Inwardly, Tadesse was preparing himself to die. Outwardly, he stated his conviction to his accusers: "The Beginner and Finisher is only God. Whatever comes, I'll accept."

In the hall, they noticed a book in his pocket. "Take it out," one yelled, and grabbed what turned out to be a New Testament. In his hands it fell open to Romans 13, within which happened to be a passage commanding obedience to authorities. "We haven't 'obeyed'; we've overthrown the Emperor," one spat out. "We are putting out reactionaries, and you are one of them."

"No, I only speak God's word, and God's word is not reactionary," Tadesse's soft voice answered.

"We don't believe in higher authorities!" they shouted back at him.

Going aside a few feet, the group whispered among themselves. "The Bible has saturated his bones," one said. "He's so devoted he cannot deny. We can't convert him or brainwash him," insisted another. The consensus was inevitable: "We must kill him, and now!"

A single bullet was the easiest way to dispose of an "enemy of the Revolution." But this embarrassingly small youth had angered them, shamed them. He seemed to have no fear. In fact, an aura of unconcerned confidence, almost pleasantness, surrounded his consistently peaceful face. Such a response was infuriating. One of them came up with a fitting method of retaliation. "Let's execute him like his hero!" He pointed to the wires above.

Back inside, they announced: "We've decided how to kill you. We'll see if your Jesus will save you. We're going to hang you on the electric wire. Take off your clothes." Tadesse obeyed. They stacked chairs on a table so that if he stood on them, he could just reach the bare electric wires hanging above. "Climb up there," they ordered him. "If Jesus was crucified on a cross, we've decided to hang you like your Jesus." The cadres were in their element, totally in control, and on the verge of eradicating this irritating little nonconformist.

The naked youth climbed up and took a footing on the top chair. He folded his arms and waited. Within himself Tadesse accepted the inevitability and the honor of such a death. After a few moments of quietness, he simply stated, "I am glad to die like this."

Two or three times in his experience with the Lord, Tadesse had seen visions similar to those recorded in the book of Acts. It was not strange to him, then, that God should visit him at such a moment. Darkness was coming on outside. Looking upward, the young stalwart saw a great light. He alone heard words spoken to him: "As I have done for the three in the fiery furnace, I will do for you."

In his spirit, Tadesse responded, "As you have done for them in their time, if you do the same now, I will go back and tell this miracle to the church. If you are calling me to die, I am willing to come to you."

Without hesitating, Tadesse took a deep last breath and reached out purposefully toward the wires. The group stood transfixed. The instant he grabbed the wires, the lights in the building went off. In confusion, someone ran outside to see if a switch had been thrown. He returned shouting, "It's dark everywhere! The electricity seems to have gone off at the main source."

"How did it go off?" they asked each other, shocked and afraid. They scuffled around in the darkness, talking in muffled tones trying to decide what to do next. Finally they ordered their victim down from the scaffold. Shaking but overwhelmed with awe, Tadesse climbed down. He awaited their next verdict.

"Your Jesus is... something...," they muttered in the darkness. "We will ... have to make another decision." Hurriedly the group came up with a face-saving alternative. With assumed bravado they gave him two terse orders: "First, go back and close your church work. Secondly, if you ever preach again, get a paper from Addis Ababa's higher authorities to do it."

Tadesse made an answer: "I cannot accept your first order, but I will accept the second, to get permission from the head office. I have permission from God."

"You stupid thing!" they retorted. "Get out!"

Tadesse swept up his clothes and dashed out the door, jubilant. He ran straight up Chencha Mountain in the darkness. Although it could well be a six-hour climb, he was so invigorated that he made it in three. Knocking at the door of the elders' council, those to whom he had sent his plea for prayer, Tadesse stood waiting. A servant came to the door and asked, "Who are you?"

"Tadesse," he answered, bursting into the room.

That night, a man who felt he was fresh out of a fiery furnace gave that amazed group of elders his testimony of deliverance. Christ had been there for him, too, the same "fourth Man" who appeared in the inferno at the three Hebrews' side. Tadesse would testify about his personal experience of God's deliverance repeatedly in the days to come, whether in prison or free. He pointed not to himself, as a near martyr on a cross, to be admired — but to God on a cross, to be worshipped.

THE AGONY OF
WAITING

"Fantaye, what is the matter with you?" her parents demanded. "Here a suitor has come asking for you again, and you are refusing this one, too. You are educated. You are well into marrying age. What is holding you back?"

Fantaye's parents were distraught. So many things about this daughter of theirs they could not understand... reading the Bible, going off on Sundays, no doubt visiting those dangerous Pentes. Yet she was a good daughter, respectful, obedient, mature. In fact, her quiet confidence in the midst of the frightening changes abroad mystified them.

Sunday by Sunday, she caught the buses necessary to make connections to the prison. The trip was an ordeal, for the whole city seemed suspicious and afraid. Bodies were no longer left on the streets, for the Red Terror had done its work. Resistance was now unthinkable. She stared out the window as they passed a hospital. Amputees from the war languished in wheelchairs or leaned on sticks in trash-strewn courtyards, staring back at the moving bus. As she hurried to another embarking point, beggars reached up from wretched rags, extending the stump of an arm, an emaciated child, or a tin can. There seemed to be so many more beggars and street children than before, so many reduced to destitution. Tired women with little ones hanging on their skirts converged at the bus stop closest to the prison. Seeing the food parcels they carried, her eyes met theirs in silent empathy.

In spite of the trip, coming was worth it, for it brought such joy to Negussie... and to Fantaye, too. The few minutes allowed them to converse over a fence between them were the highlight of her week and his.

Except for the sadness of their separation, he even seemed happy, she thought, for he was often aglow with what was happening in his "place of service." Negussie's band of believers at the prison was growing. They talked personally with other inmates and offered Bible studies when they found interest. They were short on materials, and at one point had to separate the one Bible they had into seventy parts. They developed a system of trading pages in the bathroom on Thursdays. In spite of difficulties, they were seeing a body of believers come to birth within the prison. "The Invisible Fellowship Church" they called themselves, a play on the name of the Fellowship Church that had been quite visible near the Addis Ababa University, before it was closed. Their prison church was invisible to the world, but they took pleasure in knowing their Father saw them.

Orthodox churches were still allowed to operate. Only the Lutheran-background *Mekane Yesus* Church (meaning "Place where Jesus dwells") was recognized by the government as the accepted representative of Protestantism. Ato Kaydamo's church was one non-Lutheran evangelical church inexplicably left open. Operational churches quietly made their buildings available to groups that had been closed. Outlawed groups met here one time, there another, so as not to be traceable. In the process, denominational walls were broken down, giving way to a unity of fellowship that turned out to be one of the blessings of the Revolution.

Fantaye could slip into an open church somewhere in the city, but her main spiritual support came from the underground fellowship at a home in her neighborhood. Fervent were the prayers in those meetings, for each one present had family members and friends who were in prison, at war, or in some difficulty or other. Still, there was an almost electric sense of victory among them, for they knew Whom they believed in, and trusted Him in their situations.

Whispered reports of suffering from beyond the capital became calls to prayer in the underground church. The four horses of the biblical Apocalypse seemed to be thundering over East Africa. The public at large really did not know how overwhelming the crisis was, since the government controlled the media. It was often outside journalists who leaked news out of the troubled Horn of Africa, a seething pot boiling over. Interactions between warring factions in Sudan, Somalia, and Ethiopia were triggering attacks and reprisals. The displacements they spawned worked like revolving doors. People were fanning out into homelessness in all directions, struggling to escape conscription, war, or famine.

Irony of ironies, this issue of famine which had figured strongly in the Emperor's fall in 1974 came back to discredit the new rulers a decade later. The Marxists' expensive Tenth Year Anniversary celebration overlapped the serious famine striking the Wollo region in the north, and even areas of the south.

At this same time, a curious anomaly was occurring in the heart of the north, a secret operation known to the participants as "Operation Moses." In the heart of the north near Lake Tana (source of the Blue Nile) lived an ancient Ethiopian Jewish community called "Beta Israel." These people were called "Black Jews" and were nicknamed Falashas, meaning "landless." They were the mysterious people with whom the Ethiopian Orthodox community had interacted over the centuries, resulting in what some would see as a "Judaized Orthodoxy" on the one hand, and a "Christianized Judaism" on the other. Perhaps in no other country was the Orthodox Christian Church so Jewish in custom, or the Jewish community forms so tempered by Christian influence.

Mysteriously, at given signals in 1984, some ten thousand Falashas abandoned their villages in northern Ethiopia to make a torturous month-long trek to Sudan. Along the way, an estimated one thousand perished from hardships at the hand of nature and men, whether bandits, Ethiopian troops, or Sudanese border guards. Of those who reached the camps alive, it was estimated that two to three thousand Falashas died there from dehydration and disease while waiting for secret evacuation to Jerusalem, via a Muslim land.

All this was under wraps because Chairman Mengistu, like his predecessor, barred Falasha emigration. If he were to let the Jews leave, he may have reasoned, tens of thousands of Christians, Muslims, and animists would take it as a precedent for their getting out too. In the wake of the 1984 disaster, with NBC exposing the famine and aid pouring in from the West, the flight of thousands would be embarrassing to Ethiopia's Marxist government.

The Falasha matter was delicate. Mengistu needed funds and arms for his own purposes. Military expenditures were a constant drain, and celebrations for the tenth anniversary of the Revolution would be costly — $100 million, as it was later reported. It would seem that Mengistu traded the Falashas for hidden benefits supplied through Israel. The initial cost for redeeming the Ethiopian Jews, including their first year of absorption, Israel estimated at $100 million. Through this modern Exodus, around seven thousand "Black Jews" escaped from Ethiopia, their ancestral home for possibly two or three millennia.

Of course, thousands of other Ethiopians and Eritreans had escaped to Sudan, as well. Once out, most refugees found themselves to be stuck over a border, and stateless. "Of the thousands who had fled to the camps in Sudan, the Jews were the

only ones who had a place to go — Israel — anathema to the
Communist regime," explained Ruth Gruber, author of *Rescue*.

Most Ethiopians were oblivious to the secret Falasha exodus, being themselves embroiled in the upheaval created by the
new social planning. Col. Mengistu's government declared
"villagization" to be the next strategy. Peasants were forced to
tear down their homes scattered along creek beds and rebuild
barrack-like villages up higher, supposedly to cluster them
around modern community services, which rarely materialized.

"Resettlement" was the other government scheme. Whether
their tactic of forcing people from famine areas to resettle elsewhere was really designed to improve food possibilities or, rather,
to break up centers of protest, was never clear. But some six
hundred thousand northerners were uprooted by the military
and deposited in various areas of the south. Some were dumped
in the uninhabitable tsetse fly belt, from which they tried to
escape. Wandering westward across the Sudan border, a group
from the Tigray region, for instance, ran into Sudan's civil war
zone. That meant they had to flee northward from the fighting,
also hurrying not to become cut off in the *sudd* (a broad swamp)
by the rains. When the exhausted survivors made it to a refu-
gee camp in northern Sudan, they were exposed to harsh desert
life and cholera. One night at dusk they shocked their relief
workers by silently rising up as one man and disappearing off
into the desert toward their own highlands hundreds of miles
to the east, risking death from war or famine all over again. If
they made it, their wanderings would have traced a complete
rectangle. It was hard to say the "free" were suffering less than
the imprisoned in these days of anguish.

The Ethiopian churches, although poor, did what they could
for people. Dr. Mulatu had moved to Addis after his Shashamane
ordeal and was heading up the KHC's development program. It
channeled funds from abroad and provided personnel and equip-
ment to dig wells, undertake reforestry projects, and distribute
grain. Much work was concentrated in the north, for the most

severe famine was there. On the other hand, as General Secretary of the KHC, Ato Tekle's heavy burden of care was more concentrated in the south, for that was where mission churches and schools, clinics and hospitals had been operative before the Revolution.

Into Tekle's office came reports of individual arrests and church closings. He did what he could, often pleading for someone's release or visiting them in prison. Eventually the drought struck Wolaitta too, right in the heart of the south. Wolaitta was the "parent" church to the newer congregations in remote Gamo Gofa, where so many Christians had already been imprisoned. In 1983, Tekle got word that all 738 KHC churches of Wolaitta, too, had been summarily nailed shut.

Still, God did not leave Himself without witness. Scattered evidences kept hope alive. When cadres tore the tin roof off one Wolaitta church, mysterious windstorms tore the same tin off the first and second roofs to which the cadres had nailed them. Unusual happenings shook up even the cadres, for instance the case of the cadre who swore and shook his left fist (the Marxist salute) at God as he closed the Shom'olo church in Wolaitta. The cadre went to market, drank too much, and fell down in a drunken stupor that night. That next day his remains were found. Hyenas had finished off his body, all but the identifying left fist!

Unusual things happened in the Gedeo region, too. In Dilla, first Ato Werku, the leader of the church, was imprisoned, and then sixteen head elders were arrested. The elders refused to deny Christ at their local prison, so were shipped off to distant Yavello, a loathsome prison in a dry wasteland near the Kenyan border. Repeatedly, events reminiscent of the book of Acts occurred there and elsewhere. Jailers were converted, like Paul's in Philippi. Christians were often put in charge of fellow prisoners, for their attitudes seemed to bring peace and order to angry malcontents. To say the least, prisons repeatedly were providing "a captive audience," an audience who could examine the testifiers in the hard light of a shared reality.

In the sister offices of mission and national church, Mr. Cumbers and Ato Tekle were both working night and day to guide their constituencies, to meet emergency requests, and to attend tedious court proceedings at the Ministry of Labor. Legal accusations were spawned by the slogan of the times: "Workers of the world, revolt!" Along the way, a new valve had to be placed in John Cumbers' heart in America to keep the man going, and he was told he must schedule regular monitoring outside the country. During one especially harrowing court case, Mr. Cumbers was told he could not leave the country without satisfying the court, essentially putting him under arrest. The "satisfying" was a demand for money, a demand that felt like extortion.

Such complications made administration difficult, for John was in charge of the mission's work in Sudan as well as Ethiopia. The animosity between the two nations resulted in cessation of flights between them. To get from Addis to Khartoum, the Director had to fly to Kenya and transfer to another line. Sometimes connections took days. Finally Mr. Cumbers' superiors in the International office asked him to move to Kenya to administer the East African field. John and Naomi reluctantly left. They could not know that in the 1990s, John would return to Ethiopia to collect testimonies from those Marxist years and publish them as a gift to the church. Leadership of the KHC would choose a revealing title for the book, *Count It All Joy.*

In the midst of many losses, God sent periodic encouragement. From Singapore, Pastor Yu Kwong and Lily Hseuh returned to Ethiopia for two weeks in 1984. It was Yu Kwong's fourth visit. Government regulations did not allow travel outside of Addis at the time, so clandestine meetings were arranged. This time the Hsuehs did not so much teach as just listen to the Ethiopians testify. Five or six people at a time gathered at Headquarters in the two-room apartment of Ruth Cremer, a stalwart

Bible translator from New Zealand who had an extraordinarily close relationship with the nationals. Ruth relayed their stories to the Hsuehs, hearing in various languages, and translating into English. One man told of a church whose door had been nailed shut. A ferocious windstorm tore it open, and authorities feared to close it again. Another told of an experience at Yavello prison, in the season when people were desperate for water. Unbelievers begged the Christian prisoners to pray for rain. "Not unless you repent," the believers responded. The local people did voice an honest attempt to repent. It promptly rained like a pipe from heaven on that town, but not around it. "Pastor Hsueh," one of the group emphasized with awe, "we are living in the days of the book of Acts!"

The Hsuehs returned to Asia and told believers there, "Praise God with us, for the Ethiopian Christians are doing well. They are maturing after ten years of persecution."

Negussie's prison fellowship was maturing too. His small band shared the general suffering of prison life on the physical level, but they enjoyed a freedom of spirit that transcended the walls around them. They drew many into the fellowship of the Lord Jesus Christ – around three hundred prisoners during Negussie's sojourn at Alem Buckagn. Some would eventually emerge from prison as changed people, released from bondage of body and spirit, twice freed.

During this long season of waiting, Negussie couldn't exchange letters with John Coleman, but he got word that John had taken the step they'd often wondered about when they were boys. He'd married. Negussie tried to picture John married. He learned that his teaching colleague, Mulugeta, had married too; in fact, he'd married a daughter of Ato Tekle. The old friends were in their thirties now. Negussie felt a pang of guilt as he thought of Fantaye's position. There she was, just the age to be mothering a family, and here he was, trapped, with no promise of freedom. No mechanism was even operative for prisoners to appeal their cases.

Once during that time, a thief in the prison sadistically announced to Negussie that Fantaye was pregnant. For Negussie, even the hint of such a possibility was devastating. The days before her next visit were an agony to him. He did not doubt her, yet longed for assurance from her own lips.

The Ministry of Health by now had transferred Fantaye to a position within the city, so she was living at home again. Sometimes the tension of being connected to a prisoner overcame her. *Don't risk your own safety,* a voice would say to her. But if ever she missed a Sunday, Negussie was upset.

As her family pressed her to marry and stories of endless incarcerations haunted her mind, she began to wonder whether she should just face the inevitable and let the relationship go. Over and over she pondered, *Is the strain just too much for us?*

Repeatedly she went over her prayer uttered years before, asking God for a Christian to share her life with, one who truly followed Him. She remembered her surprising assurance a month later, the very first night of their meeting, that Negussie was the person for her. *I want only the one You want for me,* she had told the Lord then, and she told Him again. As week after week ticked by, and then month after month, Fantaye held on. Another suitor came, for such was the procedure in Ethiopia. "Dating" was not the custom; a formal arrangement was usually made between families. Again, Fantaye refused the offer, to her family's dismay.

As months stretched into years, her age crept forward as the seasons passed. Negussie chastised himself for keeping her from a woman's normal entrance into marriage and motherhood. Fantaye did not know what to do. One day she finally suggested hesitantly, "Perhaps we should let the relationship go." He realized the reasonableness of her words. Yes, he knew he should allow her that freedom. He gave it.

But back home, Fantaye could not forget his having told her once, "As the land was given to Abraham, God has told me you are to be mine." She thought about God's promises to the Patriarchs. How sovereignly her Lord had brought Isaac and Rebecca together. She prayed, she agonized, but could not bring herself to break off this most precious relationship in their lives. *How very long Jacob and Rachel waited in their day, and how long must we wait?* Her soul resonated with the words of Lamentations:

> I remember my affliction and my wandering,
> the bitterness and the gall. I well remember them,
> and my soul is downcast within me.
> Yet this I call to mind and therefore I have hope:
> Because of the LORD's great love we are not consumed,
> for his compassions never fail.
> They are new every morning;
> great is your faithfulness.
> I say to myself, "the LORD is my portion;
> Therefore I will wait for him."

DELIVERANCE

Whips fell on Negussie again and again. John Coleman cringed with each blow and reached out to help him, but into thin air. John wasn't asleep, so he knew it wasn't a dream, but the scene was so vivid it electrified him.

John had been away from Ethiopia a long time. Life in Canada had become comfortable and full. *How could I have forgotten?* he asked himself. Letters from Negussie had ceased nearly seven years before. The urgency he felt in 1979 had subsided to an occasional thought or prayer. Negussie's ongoing suffering was no longer real to him, not until he was faced with it in his mind's eye.

Something snapped in John. *Here I am moving on with my life, married, about to have my first child, and my old friend is locked up and they've thrown away the key! I must do something! We can't let this go on. He has to get out!*

John was living in Saskatchewan. He immediately drove down to a federal office where people could lodge complaints and poured out his concern to an official. He asked where the former ambassador to Ethiopia was now. John remembered once going with his parents to the Canadian embassy in Ethiopia for a party the Ambassador gave for expatriates. He seemed to be a compassionate man. In fact, John thought he'd lost his whole family in an accident.

The Saskatchewan official turned to a file, dialed a number, and handed the phone to John. "Here's that man. Talk to him!" he said. John was stunned, but stammered out his concern for this friend of his who'd been in prison for years in Ethiopia for no just reason.

"You write it up, give me his name and the details, and I'll ask my successor to make discreet inquires about why he's being held." The voice gave an address and the phone clicked dead.

John went home and called his dad about the episode. "I did it so impulsively, and the official put me through instantly. Am I doing the right thing?"

Murray paused before he answered. He knew Ethiopia well. "Be careful, John, if you go through a political route. If the right official gets hold of it, it may help. If the wrong one does, they may do away with him. Go to the Lord and pray."

John did pray. But he never sent the letter. He hadn't given Negussie's name on the phone, and he never contacted the former ambassador again.

Now on the alert, however, he focused on fervent prayer for Negussie. Within a few months, unknown to him, something happened; just how or what, he never was told. Eventually the outcome reached him through a secretary at SIM headquarters.

Without warning, Fantaye's agony came to an abrupt halt. Over in Ethiopia that spring of 1986, a message came to Negussie's community: "Come to celebrate! Negussie has been freed!"

Fantaye could hardly believe her ears. "Come to celebrate?" *Yes, yes, the community always greets freed prisoners, always joins in thanksgiving and praise.* "Negussie has been freed?" *Yes, no, yes, could it be that our prayers have finally been answered? Could it be that we will next face each other with no fence between?*

Fantaye trembled as she approached Negussie's sister's home. Alemaz still did not know about Fantaye's relationship with her stepbrother. *Negussie! He will be inside. How will I ever melt into the stream of visitors who will come to greet him? Can the weight of feeling between us be kept invisible?*

People took their turns greeting the released prisoner. Her turn finally came. Fantaye found herself weeping as they embraced. It was all right, everybody embraced in Ethiopia. It was all right, everybody cried at such moments of emotion. It was all right, their secret could go unnoticed.

Fantaye's life would take on a whole new pattern now. No more Sunday trips to the prison. No more praying, *"When?"* Well, not *"When the release?"* Now it was *"When everything."* When *find a job, when be able to ...? No, we must not think too far ahead. Negussie must build up his strength. Ex-prisoners have to learn to live in freedom again. They are still suspect. Work is hard to find even for people with no mark against them. How will Negussie support himself? Let alone anyone else...*

But there was hope! There were times together. Had God not had been faithful every step of the way? Surely He could be counted upon during these special days, and for their future as well!

Of course "Jonathan and David" communicated quickly. Negussie's first letter poured out things he'd not been able to share in those eight years of silence:

July 1, 1985

My dear brother John, and your dear wife and son,

Now it seems to me as if we sit together and talk to each other. Oh! the day and time will come when we will sit face to face here on earth. I'm so eager to see you. When will it be? I'm telling my wishing that I have in my mind and keep the answer by faith.

Thank you for your lovely letter. I'm very blessed in it. I see your great love you have for me. Let God bless you and your family. I really love you. I'll never forget all our childhood times we passed together. I also know that you love Jesus, and this is why I love you. I never forget your kindness, politeness and love you have for people.

You told me that you got a wonderful Christian wife. Praise God for His unspeakable Gift. Yes! "Good gifts and perfect blessings are from the Father above." Thanks to God for your first son Jeffery. I'm very glad to have your picture. I showed it to my family.

I want to tell you briefly what you want to hear. In 1977 I started to pray for marriage. In 1979 the Lord showed me a Christian girl and I kept on praying. After four months I told her what I had in mind and let her pray for an answer. After six months she wrote to me that she got an answer, and we put our promise before the Lord. Now we are in our promise. She is a wonderful Christian. She loves the Lord and is a faithful girl. Her parents are living here in Addis. She is employed and works in Addis. Next time I hope we'll send you our picture. I told her about my family, the Colemans, and showed her all the pictures we had at Obi. She knows you and loves you. Please keep on praying for us!

John reread every word, and longed for more information.

Negussie began to move around Addis, acquainting himself with how the city's life had changed out there beyond him those seven years. Now he could stand outside the police station where he'd first been incarcerated in Addis near the Piazza. He could stand where Fantaye had stood and look into the foreboding building with x-ray eyes, picturing the layout, smelling the very stench of the place, but he stood there free. He could pass what had so long been his second Addis prison home and even still feel like a member of his old "Invisible Fellowship Church" down at "the End of the World," but he was on the outside now.

He revisited his old haunts and found the buildings largely unchanged, but much had happened to the people at each place in his absence. Most of all, he had changed. He'd suffered, grown, shared life with people and in places unknown to his old friends, and in it all he had found the Lord to be his most faithful friend. And Fantaye? She had been there with him as best she could. She was now a bridge to his past and a bridge to his future. For the present, they still had much living and learning to do together in the freedom that had abruptly come to them.

He went to find his old mentor. Pastor Kaydamo was overjoyed to see Negussie, even if he did look terrible. Kaydamo asked about Negussie's missing years, and shared what God had been doing in his own flock during them. Negussie found the *Meserete Heywet* (meaning "Foundation of Life) church to be teeming with activity. The small compound was in use day and night, since it was one of the few evangelical church facilities left open.

At the SIM compound, Negussie found the chapel burgeoning with national Christians, so many that they had to hold three services, not the single sparse service expatriates used to have there. Nightly, an underground Bible school was in full swing, having replaced GBI soon after its closing. Alex Fellows, a tough Australian bush missionary, had managed to rescue the GBI library from the sealed Jimma compound! Now Alex had come up from Soddu to take John Cumbers' role.

The Colemans had left their house out at the Press and gone home to Canada. Negussie wrote to them, including a picture, and they shared it with John, who now lived a distance from them, but still in Canada. "I think he looks quite thin as well and older," Bea wrote. "He was beaten a lot to try to get a confession out of him." Negussie's letter told the story of meeting Fantaye, and spoke simply of their long commitment to one another. Bea translated some of his Amharic, which said:

> My heart is choked up with the love and longing I
> have for you as I write this letter, and God has given me

the assurance that before we meet in heaven, we will
also see one another here on earth... She has faithfully
waited for me all this time and now we are engaged....
I have some other wonderful news, that my dear old
father has believed on Christ as his personal savior... I
am now employed in World Vision's Food and Nutri-
tion Centre. I'm a storekeeper... I long to see you and
it seems as I think of you, that all the ocean separating
us is only something one could take up in a ladle. Also
I have an ocean of things to tell you but this small ladle
full will have to suffice for this time... Please greet Sharon
and her family, Dan and his wife, Marianne and her husband. Rom. 8:18-39, Phil. 1:19-21.

Your son, Negussie

Since he was unable to visit the Colemans at their old place
at the mission press compound, he visited another friend there,
Mina Moen, who had once lived in Wolisso. Mina had taught
Amharic to missionaries over the previous three decades, yet
her deepest commitment seemed always to be with the nationals. She had a gift for helping young people know God personally and encouraging them to become faithful disciples. Negussie
was one whom she'd inspired years before. While he was in
prison, Mina had been working feverishly on something called
the "Key Scriptures" project with other linguists. They were
racing to get at least key passages translated into the vernacular
languages whose Scripture translations were in process and might
be interrupted by missionary expulsion any time. Negussie
had met some of the down-country nationals who made risky
trips to the capital to quietly work with Mina and Ruth Cremer
for weeks at a time on these tedious translations. Just out of
prison and back into the world, he was encouraged by the amazing stories these men told of what God was doing in their areas.

As Negussie and Mina talked that day in 1986, she asked
him, "Have you ever regretted taking a stand for the Lord as a
teacher, when you could have kept quiet and not used your

Bible and saved yourself from all the suffering you went through?"
After Negussie left her that day, Mina wrote down what she could
remember of his response. With a bright look, his face aglow,
he answered in this way:

> When I think of all the suffering my Lord went through
> for me, why should I be sorry for the little I could suffer
> for Him? Besides, it wasn't all in vain. When I was in
> prison, I had a captive audience and could witness much
> more freely than when I was out in the world. When the
> people saw I could rejoice in my suffering, they were
> willing to listen to me.
>
> I had so many opportunities to present the gospel,
> day after day for years! It gave time to help them not
> only to accept the Lord but also to grow in the faith.
> We had Bible studies, exchanging sheets out of the few
> Bibles we had, even in the bathroom. Of course we
> memorized passages. We formed a church in the prison,
> and even took up offerings from the bit of money we
> got from making and selling things. We sent the money
> out of prison to buy Bibles for people who didn't have
> them.
>
> No, I'm not a bit sorry I took an open stand for the
> Lord, even if it resulted in suffering, beatings, and im-
> prisonment. What a privilege was mine to be able to
> witness for my Lord as well as to suffer for Him!

Mina cherished Negussie's testimony, and often used it to challenge others in Ethiopia and abroad.

At the new KHC property, Negussie observed that the court-
yard was lined with shipping containers that looked like rail-
road cars. They had brought in relief supplies. Emptied out,
they were ideal for conversion into storage or office space. The
Development arm of the KHC was still much involved with the
famine, which had not fully abated. Dr. Mulatu negotiated with
aid organizations that focused activity on Ethiopia. Expatriate

organizations like World Vision could ship in the food, but efficient and fair distribution depended upon trustworthy nationals.

Mulugeta by now was working in the World Vision office and helped Negussie find work there. Negussie wrote John, joking about their jobs in this preparatory phase of their lives — his being a *sook tabahke* (storekeeper) and John being a *kelem kebe* (color painter), for John was painting houses in Canada. "I'll buy your *kelem* (paint) and keep it in my store...and you'll paint my house when we live together," he daydreamed. Before long, however, World Vision's project in the capital was terminated. Instead, they were made responsible for the Sekota project in the province of Wollo up north beyond Dessie.

Negussie talked with Fantaye about the possibility of his helping up there. Years before, he had told her, "I have no wealth, not much knowledge, but I have Jesus Christ in my heart, so I have everything, really. This is all I can offer you." His wealth had not increased in prison, and establishing a home would take money. Again, they must wait. Before he left Addis, however, they let their families know about their hope to someday marry. Fantaye's parents were not pleased. Even if drawn to Negussie's warm personality, they found his qualifications for her hand unacceptable, whether physical, tribal, or economic. He had a deformity; he was fathered by an Oromo, who had since died; and he had no resources. The couple knew the matter would take time, time to win her family's favor and time to afford marriage.

Meanwhile, Negussie would serve where he could. Instead of traveling north overland as he had before, he boarded World Vision's Twin Otter plane and looked down in awe on the harsh terrain, so dry and brown. Once again, Fantaye was out of reach. This time the vast expanse of the Simien Mountains lay between them.

AMBUSHED

How will we stop in time?! The little plane shook and roared as a sheer drop-off at the end of the landing strip rushed toward them. *Stabilized ...just in time!*

Negussie's first sight of Sekota had emerged from below their plane as it approached the steep-sided butte. Like everything in the Simien Mountains, this landform was stark. They'd been flying over the wrinkled face of the vast mountain range, finally spotting Sekota on the north/south road, a hundred and fifty air miles southwest of Mekele, capital of the Tigray region. Had they flown high enough to sight them, they could have seen Lake Tana gleaming in a cradle of the mountains to the west, and the escarpment dropping off abruptly into the Danakil desert, to the east.

Over the mountains south of the Sekota feeding center stood King Lalibela's magnificent churches built in the 12th century. Carved underground out of monolithic red rock, they were among the "seven wonders of the ancient world." To the southeast, Dessie Hospital lay on the Asmara road, half way between the Ethiopian and Eritrean capitals. To the west lay the Falasha settlements, their population cut in half since the "Operation Moses" exodus to Israel three years before. Every one of those destinations would take days to reach on foot. From Sekota's butte top, the eye could only view an endless circle of parched nature bathed in timeless isolation.

On arrival, Negussie reported to Ato Sahle Tilahun, the administrator. A man somewhat Negussie's senior, Sahle had a heart-shaped face, wavy hair, and a good sense of humor. His feelings easily broke through on his countenance — eyes large in a sober face, or twinkling with mirth, or widening with wonder. They darted back and forth as he talked and grew lustrous when he sensed a response to his conversation. Although he was a married man with six children, he retained a disarming simplicity, almost a naiveté, a quality not found in many these days.

During the daytime, Negussie worked as Sekota camp's stock control manager, acting as cashier and bookkeeper. When darkness fell, there was little to do but share experiences. Sahle enjoyed sharing his. Although emotionally quite involved in his own story, he maintained a kind of objectivity that came through with blunt honesty from time to time. And he could laugh at himself.

Negussie and Sahle found that they had a good bit in common. Like Negussie, Sahle had been lonely as a child, living virtually as an orphan since he was ten. Mina Moen influenced them both. She had been the language teacher at Debre Birhan when Sahle was in school there, and she'd become a spiritual mother to him. Like Negussie, Sahle had also become a teacher.

Understanding jail life was another experience Sahle and Negussie shared. Two years before the Emperor was deposed, Sahle and Aberash (later his wife) were just getting acquainted in Addis when they happened to get caught in an Orthodox-instigated police raid on a "Pente" meeting. With about 200 others, they both got thrown into Kerchaylee prison. When Negussie told stories from his prison years, Sahle could picture the place from the inside out, for he'd been there six months himself. He could still remember the shock he and Aberash had when they first spotted each other with shaved heads.Repeatedly, the two men seemed to have passed like ships in the night. Sahle and Aberash married two years after the prison term and then taught in Munz, the very place and year that the drunken man had nearly beaten Negussie to death. Most recently, Sahle had been a school director near Debre Zeit and knew the three Shoan airmen whom Negussie had met years before at the Asmara Center.

While Negussie was in his long prison years in Addis, Sahle was feeling like a prisoner himself, not formally incarcerated, but imprisoned in his principal's position in a school near Debre Zeit. Aberash managed her math teaching with fewer problems than Sahle, who had a higher profile as an administrator. Agitation to get rid of him had risen to a fever pitch in 1984. They accused him of "sowing a foreign commodity" and called him to the Party office. The night before the appointment, Sahle and Aberash pondered their predicament. "I must be happy if they put me in prison, and be thankful to the Lord," Sahle reminded his wife. Aberash assured him she was proud of his faith, and encouraged him to be bold and not ashamed.

At the Party office, they asked him questions like, "Aren't you a follower of this newcomer religion? What about your bringing this influence into the school?" They quizzed him about his political consciousness. Sahle had a fairly clear knowledge of Marxism. "I know it; I'm not ignorant of it," he insisted, challenging the Party men in return. Years earlier he'd done his two-week Marxist indoctrination course that teachers were required to take. He'd even been sent back a second time for "remedial training," since the stubborn man did not seem to acquiesce.

When a higher Party leader came to Debre Zeit, about 4,000 people assembled in a big warehouse for a meeting called to expose the "Pentes." Sahle was one of the accused. After kebele reports, the harangue began. The ordeal lasted from nine to three.

"What are the characteristics of this newcomer religion?" the leader asked, rhetorically. Response: "It fools students, tells them not to fight, to throw guns down and pray. They say if we pray, money will come through the roof of the house. But the Orthodox people go to war and even take the *Tabot* (Ark). The Orthodox are patriots! This new religion is the opposite. Our school director invites students by night and indoctrinates them. He is our enemy! We can't separate him from the imperialists!"

Sahle had long had the habit of trusting God with childlike faith. He observed the vicissitudes of his own life with amusement, as if looking on from the outside. He chuckled mischievously when telling Negussie about this meeting where he was squirming in the hot seat:

"I was fanning myself while I was sitting in the audience. *Today I'm going to get it,* I thought. Then I noticed I was fanning myself with a magazine...oh, oh...Guideposts Magazine, published by Christians in the USA. I thought, *I can't swallow it! I can't throw it down. I brought my own evidence!* I tell you I was really sweating.

"They assigned students to make accusations. 'Ato Sahle has done this, done that,' they went on. 'Have him go to Marxist discussions,' was a recommendation. 'No,' the cadres threw back, 'he knows, he's denied Marxism as a science. We can't say he's ignorant. You try to convince him!' The meeting ended with me being condemned and publicly cursed aloud."

After that, Sahle had to move the family off the school compound. It was the rainy season and two of their children had the measles. Just when he'd managed the resettling with difficulty, they were told to move again. Alas, next they put Sahle in jail at the kebele prison.

"It was really very funny," he told Negussie. "It was a shock for the town to have the principal sleeping on the ground in jail right at sixth and eighth grade exam time. When report cards were due, I had to pay bail and get out just to get my reports done!"

Things deteriorated further. Where to live next? A couple in Debre Zeit kindly offered the large family their small service house — two narrow rooms, one about nine feet square, the other slightly larger, with the usual cooking shed outside. Sahle loaded up their goods and settled the family there. They enrolled their children in the Debre Zeit schools. Meanwhile Sahle had to walk ten kilometers a day to his own school.

Soon the educational authorities and kebele officers decided to strip Sahle of his principalship. They arranged to send him to a common teacher's job at a small school in a distant area. He'd been a school director for four years directing two shifts of grades one to eight. "I tell you, we were broken into pieces. We'd just paid school fees for our own children to start the new term in Debre Zeit in September. *How many times more with no house, no position?* we wondered. We were utterly broken."

They went to appeal the matter to the education office. Aberash was weeping as she faced the man in charge: "If you can't decide the truth...if your decision is illegal and not right...then our heavenly Father will make the right decision," she flatly stated.

"It's Sahle's mistake," the manager said.

"How so?" she retorted.

"He didn't register as a Party member!"

"I'm very glad he isn't a registered member," she returned.

"Aberu (his loving nickname for her), let it be," Sahle hushed her. "Please cool down, relax, take it easy. It's not the end of our life!"

One Party man saw the truth of the situation and tried to intercede for them, but officials left the thing hanging in the air. In Debre Zeit, believers from a number of church groups were praying for this beleaguered couple, including Girma, Teshome, and Solomon's families.

Very soon, help arose from an unexpected quarter. When the letter came, Sahle virtually jumped with joy. "Aberu," he shouted, "World Vision is asking me to join them! And to start in two weeks!" Had he still been a principal, getting a "free letter" to leave his post would have been difficult to obtain; jobless, he was free to go.

Sahle was not one to hold a grudge and he could always see the humor in a situation. He chucked telling the next episode: "When I began working for World Vision in the south, I had to travel through Debre Zeit in a big station wagon. I worked a half a year in Wolaitta, then in Kambatta. As my old accusers would see me drive through, they'd say, 'We are ashamed.' I tried to pray for them instead of cursing them. I prayed especially for about ten Party people after I came north here to Sekota. When I go home on leave, I even take bananas and go to visit them. Before, we were quarreling. Now I am hugging them. We are reconciled. The Lord can change things. He is a miraculous God! Some of them admitted to me, 'Sahle's God is the true God.'"

Negussie enjoyed the nightly stories, but the ravages of famine and war demanded the World Vision staff's utmost attention in the daylight hours. Sekota town's location was precarious, for it was circled by the Derg army, and farther out, circled again by the Tigray People's Liberation Front. The rebels were desperate for supplies too, which put stores of food in jeopardy. For three years there had been little rain. People would walk long distances to get food from the center. Among those who came were Agau people, a distinct ethnic group who ruled Ethiopia before the Solomonic line, and included the Falashas.

Since Negussie and Fantaye were now engaged, they eventually arranged for her to visit him on her annual thirty-day leave. She held her breath as the supply plane nosed down to land on the 900-meter butte. On the ground, she felt uneasy knowing the Ethiopian Army and a ring of the TPLF guerrillas surrounded them. She helped where she could and saw more suffering than she'd yet seen. Still, it was good to be in the same location with Negussie. After her visit, letters followed.

One day, however, riveting news came over Fantaye's radio. And having gone back to Addis on home leave that week, Sahle heard it too. "Sekota is ambushed," the radio blared. "The TPLF has taken the town!" Sahle was shocked. He could hardly believe it. He'd missed being caught by only three days and was sitting safely at home!

After waiting anxiously for over two weeks for word about the camp's fate, people learned the details: The rebels had brought 500 mules and donkeys and loaded up World Vision's stores of wheat, flour, oil, and the like. They held the World Vision staff under house arrest for fifteen days, while the hungry fighters enjoyed eating the food on hand.

They needed cash, too. Negussie told Mulugeta at World Vision's head office later that when the guerrillas demanded money, it came into his mind, *This is God's money. It was given for the destitute. I don't want to give it to the rebels.* Negussie boldly refused to hand anything over. "We have nothing to give you. You have taken all our supplies, and we don't have money to give to you." He refused to discuss it further and was willing to take the consequences. They surprised him. They refrained from resorting to further pressure.

During the two weeks, they gave the famine workers daily political consciousness classes, talking about democracy and their goals.   Then they gave the captives four rather magnanimous choices: go abroad, go back home, stay in the area, or join the TPLF. It seemed that the TPLF at first hoped simply to get the Tigray province free from the Derg.   That was their goal when Sahle and Negussie were at Sekota. Later *Yehadig* (the wider coalition of fronts) decided to try to defeat the Derg and take leadership of the whole country.

After holding them captive for fifteen days, some of the rebels escorted the workers out. They walked with them three days, exhausting days of climbing up and down the rippling mountain expanse. Negussie had kept the money in hiding, and carried it out. He was not in condition for such physical exertion and it took all his strength. About three hours short of Korem, a town on the Dessie road under Derg control, the TPLF escort bid them a cordial good-bye and left the group to make their way on alone. In Korem, they could find transport to Addis.

Back in Addis, Negussie went to the World Vision office. It was nearly Christmas. He took every cent of the money he had carefully protected from capture. They appreciated and respected him, "but his reward," Mulugeta lamented, "was simply to end up jobless."

ANOTHER
WORLD OPENS

For nearly six months, the ex-prisoner was jobless. At least he and Fantaye had more time to see each other. He wrote to John as 1987 closed, comforting him about some difficult times John had written he'd been going through, and reaffirming their mutual affection. Negussie tried to see things from God's point of view.

> I never forget you and you always live in my heart. I also feel your great and deep love that you have for me. Even though we live in different countries and very far from each other, we always live before and in the Lord, so that we see each other through faith and prayer by one Spirit.

From time to time Negussie was employed as an English/ Amharic translator or as an individual tutor at the mission language school that year. Students loved him. He was such a warm, cheerful fellow that they may not have realized what he'd been through. Sometimes they would tease him about being a bachelor. He would smile and say little in response to that subject.

Development work was a temptation to turn to. Yet that did not fit with his personal sense of calling. One of the church's serious problems during the famine years was a growing dependence upon financial assistance from abroad. Not only did this phenomenon diminish local church initiative and responsibility, it also tended to divide believers into two camps, those engaged in "spiritual" ministry, and those in "development." The two budgets showed a vastly different pay scale. While the struggling Bible schoolteacher walked almost everywhere, the development worker roared around in the project's vehicle.

What Negussie longed for was further training. He thought of his old friends' situations. Many had married. John Coleman had finished college and had become a pastor and even a father of a child, little Nathan. Negussie tried to picture their lives. He waited. He kept praying that God might open up study for him, abroad.

Might there be a chance? A slight sense of thawing seemed to be in the air. Marxist Party line and Mengistu's tough bravado were wearing thin, even among the leadership. The civil war dragged on, unresolved. An Ethiopian who returned from abroad used the words of Pharaoh's counselors in Moses' time to summarize the economic situation: "Egypt is ruined." Party regulations relaxed a little and a few travel permits were being issued. Pastor Kaydamo even got an exit visa to travel to Israel. The trip was funded by an individual who understood the significance of Ethiopia's Jewish roots and what it could mean to a Christian expositor to experience the Holy Land.

Underground, the church stirred like a smoldering volcano. Great numbers of people had come to Christ during these years of desperation. They were maturing and were ready to tell the world where to find hope. The Great Commission (the Ethiopian name for Campus Crusade) guided a network of a thousand underground Bible study cells in Addis, in well-organized synchronization. In these groups, people found their unity in Christ, despite old tribal prejudices. Wonder of wonders, the Commission's leader was himself an Eritrean.

Out at the Debre Zeit and Bishoftu area, a beehive of activity swirled. The church born in the little cottage on the edge of the lake had burgeoned into a big community. The three airmen administered a fine underground night Bible school in their adjacent homes in town. From New Zealand, SIM called back Bruce Bond, the veteran horticulturist who had developed the Shashamane Leprosarium farms, to spearhead a "food for work" reforestation project on the lake's edge. Contrary to all previous policies, the government allowed the KHC to initiate an orphanage and development project at a neighboring lake, called Kuriftu. Both lakeside ministries made significant contributions to public service. Furthermore, Christians who came there for conferences were strengthened. Years later, an Ethiopian leader avowed, "The mission's greatest contribution during the Revolution was Bishoftu — a Godsend to the national church, *all* the churches — the one protected place we found to gather, grow, and become one."

The exponential multiplication of believers of all denominations in the country demanded far more pastoral care than was available. Negussie participated helpfully in Pastor Kaydamo's congregation, but felt the need for more training. The church compound teemed with activity day and night. The small enclosure tucked into a thickly populated midtown area was about half a football field's size, and was tightly constricted by the road in front and homes or storefront shops on three sides. In the center of the compound a rectangular two-story sanctuary stood, with church offices, classrooms, and meeting rooms on the lower floor. A long row of rooms along the north wall of the compound housed the administrative and literature department offices, plus a series of classrooms — packed daily, for they served as elementary school classrooms as well. There was barely turn-around roadway and parking for a few cars inside the enclosure. Of course, not many Ethiopians owned cars. Since the government had closed the *Meserete Christos* ("Christ the Foundation," Mennonite-background) and many other churches that were not Orthodox or Lutheran, Kaydamo's congregation absorbed others. The various entities used the accommodations in relay fashion, day and night.

Although missions maintained skeleton staffs in Ethiopia, the few missionaries remaining in the country had to stay away from these national churches, for their presence threatened the national Christians with being accused of "fraternizing with capitalists." Getting to be present in a national service was a rare gift. Nearly every Ethiopian in these national congregations was going through suffering of some kind — a son killed in the war, a teenager denied educational advancement as a "Pente," one's limb lost in battle, harassment in the workplace or no work at all. Everywhere life was sobered by hunger, illness, poverty, loneliness, and death. These shared burdens drew people together into a previously unknown unity. At certain periods in the service, the congregation prayed — all at the same time — in low tones that undulated softly across the congregation as people knelt at their benches. The rare expatriate who was allowed to attend described the sense of the Spirit of God hovering over the congregation, whose tears of love and joy overflowed so naturally that the reality of God's presence was palpable.

Although missionaries had to keep their distance, they tried to help unobtrusively in what ways they could. Literacy work was one endeavor the government still allowed. Assisting the national churches' relief and development initiatives was another. But of all the swelling church's requests, leaders begged most for *training* — for leadership development. They knew Jesus developed people, not programs.

As Negussie used his own gifts for the good of the community, Pastor Kaydamo, Ato Tekle, Dr. Mulatu and other leaders recognized the young man's potential. Such men were rare. One day Negussie was called in and told that the KHC was offering him a scholarship to study at Scott College in Kenya! This would qualify him for further church leadership, a future to which he could look with great expectations. Undergirded with prayer, Negussie went to apply for an exit visa, a permission that the government often blocked. The joy cry went up when it came through.

Thrilled as they were about the opportunity, Fantaye and Negussie had to steel themselves, for this meant postponing marriage further. Still, the promise of a settled career did give the couple solid hope for the future.

By now, they'd waited a decade. Again, they parted. Fantaye watched his jet disappear into the sky. Those who got out of Ethiopia in those tense days could not help feeling a surge of relief. For Negussie, school in Kenya opened up a whole new world. For Fantaye, it meant daily perseverance in the same old world. Now Negussie would have to remember Fantaye's rich, soft voice as he read her letters over the next fifteen months. This time the barrier was not a fence, not a mountain range, but a national boundary.

CONSUMMATION

John Coleman thanked God when a letter arrived from Negussie bearing a Kenyan stamp! He tore it open and scanned the hastily scribbled lines:

> Never forget the love we are tied up to each other is the same as David and Jonathan... I was in hard and challenging years to set up my future life. I was before God in my place waiting for Him till He comes to move forward where He wants me to go or be...The time was getting longer to marry my fiancée, no house even to rent, no constant job. I'd lost and left everything for the Lord's sake, which is great gain for me I count! No answer from the earth, so faithfully waiting from above the mighty God. Yes, answers are there. Is. 40:27-30. Answer came, and now I am in Scott Theological College in Kenya, which is 64 km. away from Nairobi, from May 2, 1989. My fiancée is in Ethiopia and we'll pass to 12 years of engagement. Pray for us.

The next letter was full of enthusiasm for classes and described the beauty of the college's setting. "The only problem is", he joked, "I can't get *injera* and *doro* (chicken) *wut* . For the first time after three months I had it in Nairobi two weeks ago. I hope when Fantaye comes, she will prepare me some."

1989 passed into 1990. John wrote Negussie about some very difficult things in his life at that time, and Negussie wrote back tenderly to encourage him:

> When I was in prison, I was sick and almost I was about to transfer to the glory of His presence. I thought it was the last breath, and I with deep breath said, 'Lord, is it the last time I finish my earthly course and come to you? Thank you, for I will come and see your face!' It did not happen as I thought, but now I am here, even preparing for the ministry ahead of me. It is even the time when we feel that we are not fit, or are not strong, that the Lord uses in a mighty way. Be encouraged, my beloved brother!

In the next six months, one barrier to the couple's union after another arose. Means of support was a problem. An exit visa was another hurdle. Negussie wrote:

> Fantaye is still waiting for God's time to come out.... The Ministry of Health is the one who refused to permit her out. But since there are many changes in Ethiopia, she is hoping to join me in April. Please keep up praying with us... God called us to His ministry and she is by faith starting to send her goods... Thank you for your sweet Amharic greeting. I hope you will teach Phyllis as well, so when we meet, God willing, Phyllis and Fantaye will greet each other. Maybe one day you will come to Ethiopia or we will come to Canada and visit each other. Yes, we will prepare you nice *injera b'wut* and you will enjoy it!"

April 1990 came and went. Negussie started his second year's classes and kept praying. Months went by before the breakthrough came.

A flood of conflicting emotions swept over Fantaye as she embraced her family at the last public gate of the Addis Ababa airport and went on alone through the gate marked "Nairobi."

"How can you quit such a good job?" they had argued. "How can you choose such a man?" Nevertheless, Negussie had respected Ethiopian custom and commissioned his brother to take three community elders to Fantaye's family to secure their permission, however grudging it might be. Although the parents had made it clear that her choice was displeasing to them, she loved the family that had cradled her. Now she was flying off into the unknown, to a foreign country, to an unknown future. But central to that future was Negussie. She had prayed and waited for so long. The time had come.

All during the thousand-mile flight, she continued to pray and prepare herself. In Nairobi, her bridegroom waited. It was Scott College's 1990 Christmas vacation, allowing him time to help his fiancé settle briefly into a place in Nairobi to prepare for their marriage, while he prepared for her arrival in Machakos.

Although missing the presence of their families, the couple was not without guests for their wedding. The Ethiopian Diaspora in Kenya knew each other through the Ethiopian Fellowship Church that met in the Kenya International Conference Center, but they needed a larger place for this wedding. Pastor Berhanu arranged for the sanctuary of the large Nairobi Baptist Church. Negussie had often assisted Pastor Berhanu in Christian meetings. The groom was well known and deeply loved. Business and professional people, students and refugees wanted to celebrate with the couple that day. They came bearing gifts, film for the photos, food for the reception, cars for the parade — whatever supplies the all-day celebration required. "We've never seen such a wedding," they raved afterward.

There is something about an Ethiopian marriage ceremony, even when performed in a foreign country, which defies description. It's not the ceremony itself, it is the majestic grace with which Ethiopians tend to carry themselves, almost as if King Solomon and the Queen of Sheba's court were at hand. The traditional Ethiopian bride's cape is embroidered with gold and her dignified head is crowned with gold as well. She is clothed in spotless white.

For Christians, the ceremony pictures deep biblical expectations. It points forward to the ultimate marriage toward which history is moving. That consummation glimpsed in the book of Revelation is issued in by "the Marriage Feast of the Lamb." The Son of God receives his Bride, whom He has purchased with his own blood and whom He has been preparing for entrance into this new phase of life. All the peoples of the earth are invited to this ultimate wedding which will draw people together from all time and space, all those who have loved the Son.

As that crowd of people came together at the church in Nairobi, their skins of different hues were representative of the awaited Marriage Feast. Some did not know each other. Most came to Negussie's wedding because of their relationship to the bridegroom. Fantaye herself really knew almost no one at her wedding, except the groom and Pastor Berhanu, and yes, Sahle. Typical of Sahle's happy fortune, he happened to be sent to a conference in Nairobi at just the right time.

Thanksgiving overflowed as the newlyweds at last set up a home together. On December 3, 1990, Negussie wrote John as a married man. He gave a few details of the wedding and Fantaye's presence was reflected in all he wrote:

> Fantaye is cooking, and sometimes coming to sit for a while... How it will be wonderful when we two families could be together!...We thank you for your lovely card and the enclosed money... Yes! Our Lord is faithful so at the end of our years of engagement, at His own time, God accomplished everything for us. God gave us sweet life, happy home and rest. We thank you for your faithful prayers and let us rejoice together for the Lord has done such great things for us.

Negussie was in the midst of his second year at Scott. These were happy days. After classes, sometimes they would take walks or picnics in the cool of the evening. At home, he would strum his guitar and sing in the night hours, enjoying Fantaye's presence. He loved a song about *El-Shaddai* (God Almighty) by an Ethiopian singer named Derege Kebede. One line expressed: "In my own strength, I'd not have gotten through. God's grace got me through." As Negussie sang, he remembered all he had weathered. The decade before, his guitar had brought him difficulty, for they tried to force him to sing for the Revolution. Now he could sing to his God and his wife in peace. "The difficult days are over," he would say to Fantaye. "The future lies ahead. Don't be afraid. A time of blessing is ahead of us."

Three men from Wolaitta were studying at Daystar College in Nairobi, and the couple would sometimes go to the city and visit their apartment. When one of the roommates would get up to prepare tea, Fantaye would tease him saying, "Ethiopian men don't prepare tea!" "But you don't know where the supplies are," he'd counter. "Oh yes I do!" she'd insist, and take over in the kitchen. On special days, the delicious aroma of red pepper *wut* wafted from the stove.

"How we enjoyed being with them," one of the men said later. "Their relationship was beautiful; words can't express it. She'd gone against her family and lost her good job to marry Negussie. Her brothers found it hard to accept a deformed person and they tried to isolate her if she married him. Losing her job was costly, but she said she preferred being Negussie's wife to her position at the Ministry of Health."

During this period, the German nurse who had awarded Negussie his first Bible in Wolisso made a visit to the newlyweds. Chris Ott had treasured Negussie's letters, especially the one in which he said, "I have chosen the path of the cross, to glory." Married now herself, Chris arranged to see Negussie and his bride in Nairobi. She was relieved that his suffering was over and was now replaced with opportunities for meaningful service and graced with the joys of married life.

In May of 1991, just as Negussie was starting his third year at Scott, his letter to John shared exciting news: "For some time Fantaye was not feeling good, and I was a bit concerned. Now she is doing well and praise the Lord for that. She is pregnant and we are expecting a baby!"

As Negussie and Fantaye expectantly awaited the birth of their first child, people back at home waited expectantly too, as Ethiopia paused precariously before a ripening dawn.

THE NOOSE
TIGHTENS

Watching the news, Negussie and Fantaye could see that time appeared to be running out for Mengistu's government. It was 1991, and all over the communist bloc, regimes and symbols had been going down like a stack of cards. First came Poland's Solidarity movement, then the fall of the Berlin Wall, Czechoslovakia's "velvet revolution," the violent suppression of protesters in China's Tiananmen Square, and Romania's revolution wrought by prayer. The world watched their televisions in amazement as Lenin's mute and prone statue was lifted by helicopter and dumped.

During these years, military funding had been drying up for Ethiopia. Gorbachev told Mengistu that the Kremlin, which from 1977 to 1989 had poured a total of eleven billion dollars into Ethiopia's war economy, would not renew its military treaty with Addis Ababa when it ran out in 1991. Cuba terminated twelve years of military cooperation with Mengistu.

One country increased rather than decreased negotiations. In spite of Ethiopia's having broken diplomatic relations with Israel in 1973, the Jewish nation had quietly supplied various sorts of military aid, spurred on by their stake in the strategic Red Sea region and Zionist hopes for rescuing the rest of Beta Israel. Now Israel stood in the wings, waiting.

Cracks in Ethiopia's solidarity were widening. Massive disruptions and loss of life through war, famine, and displacement fanned the populace's determination to get relief. The Eritreans held out in their war of secession, seemingly unbeatable. Just below Eritrea but within Ethiopia lay the Tigray region. In the late 1980s, the liberation front of Tigray (the TPLF) had moved forward as a formidable enemy to Mengistu's regime. By 1989, the Tigray, Oromo, and Amhara fronts decided to consolidate their forces. They named their coalition "the EPRDF," the Ethiopian People's Revolutionary Democratic Front. By 1990, they controlled most of Tigray, and in 1991 launched three offensives that virtually destroyed the Ethiopian army. Steadily they marched on through the Gondar and Gojam regions, and took sections of Wollega and Wollo.

Diaspora Ethiopians in Kenya and all over the world held their breath when the report came on May 20th that the EPRDF had captured all the government positions in northern Shoa, had taken Ambo (less than 50 miles north of Wolisso), and were advancing on the capital. Demoralized and fleeing troops were all that lay between the coalition forces and Mengistu's headquarters in the capital. Sensing the noose tightening around his neck, the dictator fled the country by small plane on May 21st.

By the 23rd, Lenin's huge statue no longer stood in the capital, the red flag with its hammer and sickle no longer flew over Revolution Square, and Mengistu's picture was disappearing from government offices. In the midst of this vast turn-around, the Ethiopian armed forces disintegrated. They began selling their weapons and robbing civilians. Some soldiers went home. Many officers fled to Sudan, Djibouti, or Kenya. Naval units dispersed across the Red Sea.

That last week, the EPRDF dealt strategically with the seat of government, capturing the air force base at Debre Zeit (near Bishoftu) first. Ethiopian airmen feared for their lives. Yehadig soldiers rounded up sixty officers in the middle of Debre Zeit town, and made them await their fate. Some local believers took pity on them and began supplying the prisoners with food. Many of the airmen expected to be killed and some were uniquely open to the risen Lord's invitation to come to Him for eternal life. Staying among them to offer that invitation were the three Air Force brothers, Girma, Solomon, and Teshome. After a few days, the captors sorted out junior officers and gave them permission to go, but the fate of senior officers remained unknown. So many had staked their lives on Christ in those short days, that by their own choice Girma, Solomon, and Teshome took the risk of remaining among the waiting prisoners, in order to strengthen them and tend to their new brothers' needs.

In Kenya, Negussie and Fantaye strained to hear every word on BBC. Had Addis Ababa been taken? No! An unprecedented interruption was making history, somewhat like Joshua's seven-day walk around Jericho. While government troops guarded the perimeter of the Addis international airport, rebel forces halted in a circle eighteen kilometers outside the capital. For three days, Addis was left untouched. In their homes, people kept waiting in fear of what was coming. Many were fervent in prayer. Overhead, hour after hour the scream of jet after jet split the sky. Why?

In that strange pause between Friday, May 24th, and Sunday, the 26th, an operation code-named "Solomon" was taking place. This was another astounding chapter in the Falasha saga.

It so happened that Israel had been furnishing an array of military assistance to Ethiopia in exchange for permitting the emigration of the remnant of Beta Israel. Some Falashas remained in Ethiopia after the 1984 Operation Moses airlift from Sudan. In May 1991, Israel had paid Mengistu US $35 million in cash for his clearance to fly the Black Jews who had gathered in Addis Ababa to Israel.

When the last of forty plane sorties had landed in Israel, the lid came off. The *Jerusalem Post* headlines announced: "ETHIO-PIAN JEWRY RESCUED! 14,400 ARE FLOWN HERE IN A 24-HOUR LIFT." Negussie could read it in Kenya, Colemans in

Canada, and everywhere Ethiopians were scattered, a cry of amazement went up.

Operation Solomon was accomplished without panic. As if guided by a master plan, both the Ethiopian soldiers and the TPLF forces paused for three disciplined days, just long enough for this historic event's completion. The rescue planeloads included a world record, one thousand passengers on one Jumbo jet, a cargo flight with no seats. "You could never do it with pudgy Russians and Israelis with five suitcases in each hand," a bus driver told the *Post.* "They are thin, these Ethiopians."

As soon as Beta Israel was gone, Yehadig pulled the noose tight. By now Sahle and Aberash lived out on the west edge of Addis, where they began to sight tanks in their area. They'd finally been able to build an adequate home and they feared it would be demolished. They watched and prayed as the tense hours ticked past. At dawn on the 28th, Sahle noticed the Ethiopian troops moving about their nearby encampment passively, shaving and combing their hair as smoke arose in the distance from the palace grounds. Later in the day, they'd fire straight up in the air to get the attention of those passing by. "Hey! Do you want to buy something? A door? A fridge? An AK 47 or a hand grenade for a bargain price? Come and buy!" In contrast, the battle-weary TPLF swept in with long, uncombed hair framing determined faces.

Then the fireworks really let loose. Sahle and Aberash gathered their children under their bed. The whole world seemed to be collapsing, with Derg tanks shooting and rifle fire ripping the air. Theirs had consistently been a praying and singing family. They'd not prayed and sung in this context before! Singing steadied their hearts and helped to drown out the three-hour din. "The Lord is my shepherd...," they read from Psalm 23, words they had never experienced in such a setting.

Bruce Adams by then had taken over the reins of the mission from Alex Fellows. He said it all happened so much more quickly and neatly than could have been anticipated. The battle for the city that morning of May 28th met little resistance. At 5 am, the TPLF's tanks with big guns started moving up Churchill Boulevard toward the Old Palace grounds where the Derg supporters made their last stand. From the Headquarters vantagepoint, the expatriates could see smoke rising from the direction of the Presidential Palace as shells exploded and an ammunition dump blew up. It was an uncanny experience, Mr. Adams said. "The HQ community could hear the gunfire while we were gathered around a radio listening to a BBC correspondent who was reporting it from the Hilton Hotel just across the city, in plain view."

Up north in Eritrea, the EPLF had taken Dekemhare, Keren, Asmara, and the port at Assab. With the fall of Addis to the EPRDF, the EPLF announced they now considered Eritrea to be a self-governing region. A referendum regarding secession would be conducted, they said. The solidarity of Ethiopia was breaking up.

As news of the Marxist government's defeat spread across the realm, reactions varied. Some thanked God the ordeal was over, others descended into bitterness as they saw their dream disintegrate. Ali Musa, the brutal tyrant who had terrorized Gamo Gofa, shot himself.

When "reckoning time" inevitably arrived in the long established communities across the land, crooked officials during the Marxist regime were in trouble. A rare "Joseph" stood out. A man from Hadiya typified the experience of those who had ruled justly. "When the TPLF overpowered the Mengistu government in 1991," he recounted later, "the administrators ran away, fearing reprisals from the people. I stayed where I was. Some friends asked me, 'Why don't you take your family and flee for your life?' I replied that the Lord had called me to this job and was able to protect me under any circumstances. When the new government finally got around to investigating me, they asked the people of the district what sort of administrator I had been. Not one person testified against me."

Such was a loving God's answer to the praying community who had undergirded that administrator. Stalwart lives like this man's pointed to the only One who really could enable weak humans to become the unselfish "new humanity" that Marxism had so confidently hoped to create. As a Bulgarian believer had expressed from prison years before, "Although derided, persecuted, and hidden away, the Christian in a Marxist society is simply called to *be* the new man communism vainly hoped to produce — the kind of man only Christ can be, living in his people."

The Christian community had stood firm. They reverberated with David's praise in the 66th Psalm:

Praise our God, O peoples, let the sound of his praise be heard; he has preserved our lives and kept our feet from slipping. For you, O God, tested us; you refined us like silver. You brought us into prison and laid burdens on our backs. You let men ride over our heads; we went through fire and water, but you brought us to a place of abundance... Come and listen, all you who fear God; let me tell you what he has done for me.

BRIGHT HORIZONS

Excited as they were, it was difficult to be alone in a foreign country without the customary care that usually surrounded a birth in Ethiopia. Fantaye went for the delivery to an African Inland Mission hospital outside the capital, at Kijabe. No family members were at hand to give the customary bed care to mother and child in the hospital. The couple's loneliness was relieved somewhat by the kind ministrations of the daughter of Soddu Hospital's administrator, from Ethiopia. She happened to be studying in Moffat Bible College, also located at Kijabi. Meseret broke away from her studies night by night to help Fantaye.

Negussie wrote John and Phyllis on August 20th announcing the birth of their child:

> Praise the Lord!.... Name Nathanael — Gift of God. ...We have got a baby boy...He is a very quiet and lovely boy. Once he is feeding at the breast, no complaining. It is very interesting to watch him and really we like the ways he is acting and trying to communicate his feelings... We received your check. May God bless you for your love and great concern you have for us. It was on our need time. You know what we've said, when we feel, you also feel at the same time, because you allow your heart, mind and prayer to connect to ours. God is

so faithful and we are a very happy family.

After the delivery, Meseret sometimes went to visit the family at Machakos. She watched how kindly Negussie treated his wife, undertaking things strictly left to women in their culture. He helped his wife carry her load by shopping for food and household supplies, changing diapers and bathing the baby, and even cooking when Fantaye was not well. *What a wonderful husband,* Meseret observed. She knew where such love came from, yet custom usually held its expression in check even in Christian families at home.

The family sometimes invited fellow students at Scott into their home to enjoy *injera* and *wut* with them. They held Negussie in high respect. They saw the couple's classless kind of love. Negussie and Fantaye gave the young girl they employed in their home her food before they ate.

This marriage was based on a threefold friendship between each other and the Lord. They regularly prayed and studied the Scriptures together. At night, when Negussie knelt in prayer alone, Fantaye felt secure under his headship and mused, *How marvelously God has answered the prayer of my youth.* So many things were finally happening. Marriage, parenthood, and Negussie's future ministry were finally becoming realities. Praise and thanks filled their hearts to overflowing.

News from home was so encouraging that they felt led to encourage John about his future as well. They all were hoping their lives could finally converge.

Now in Ethiopia it is peaceful. The provisional government allowed all churches to function... At Wolisso churches grew from five to thirteen. These eight new churches were born underground. There are similar results in all the churches in Ethiopia. The time is at hand, we need you to come to Ethiopia to join us. Yes! ... we will pray about it.

Ato Kaydamo had invited Negussie to come to do a five-month internship at the Meserete Heywet Church as one of his final year's course alternatives. For weeks they prepared for the trip. Still conditioned by memories of the old Marxist oppression, they disembarked in Addis with a tinge of fear.

How changed they found the atmosphere to be! When the Derg went down, the underground church burst into the open. The Mennonite-background church had grown a hundredfold. One Full Gospel church's first open service brought 15,000 people. Of course the Lutheran-background Mekane Yesus Church had remained open and had grown greatly as well. Kaydamo's Meserete Heywet church had so mushroomed that the elders decided to multiply it into eleven congregations spread across neighborhoods over the city. From then on, the founding church was just called "Geja" for its neighborhood.

Among the Geja church leaders was Negussie's previous mentor, Ato Tekle, who had served as General Secretary of the KHC until 1986. Then Tekle had stepped down to become Church Growth Secretary while Dr. Mulatu moved into the KHC's national head position. Negussie learned from elders like these men who were serving the Christian community. He left home early and returned home late, working with small groups and doing personal counseling.

The Colemans had returned to Ethiopia after the Derg fell. They were overjoyed to see Negussie after all those years and to meet his lovely wife and child. Nathanael had been born in August. Murray and Bea told the couple how they had shared their story and had asked people in Canada to pray for them. Canadian French-speaking missionaries, named Jean and Soula Isch, had especially prayed. They had taken a photo of the hat John treasured — the woven white hat with the green design that Negussie had made for John in prison. Murray and Bea gave the Kumbis news of John's family. All this stirred Negussie's hope that John could someday come home.

Negussie's friend from Wolisso years, Mulugeta, was still working with World Vision in Addis. With him Negussie shared the vision for service that was developing in his mind. He felt there was a lack of counseling in the church. Young and old struggled with spiritual and material problems. Conditions in Ethiopia had been crushing. Evangelists preach and then move on, Negussie observed, but his was a concern for someone to pay attention to people's problems, to listen to them, pray with them, and help them in practical ways.

During his internship he trained some 120 leaders of small group Bible studies and prayer fellowships which were flourishing in the branch churches. The main Geja church had grown to over 3,000 members and a ministry staff of a dozen. Negussie spoke successively at the thirteen branch churches, revised Sunday school curriculum, and started a counseling ministry.

While back in Ethiopia, relationships with relatives were important for the young family to develop. A grandchild could not fail to soften the hearts of Fantaye's parents, even though they had been loath to see the two marry. Nathanael was a beautiful child, the image of his father, minus any deformity. As for Negussie's family, his half-sister and half-brother had gone to Addis almost before he could remember, and there were bridges to build with them too in adulthood. Alemaz practiced Orthodoxy devoutly. There were talks about the faith, not always reaching agreement, but she admired and loved her brother dearly. It was good for Negussie to relate to his older brother, now a businessman in Addis.

The future looked brighter for Ethiopia, the church was above ground, and expatriate missionaries were even getting entry visas. Negussie knew that John Coleman had hoped to return to Ethiopia, and he wondered when they might really meet again. Might their children play together one day, as they once played in the woods at Obi?

After the internship, the Kumbi family returned to Kenya. Negussie launched into his final year of studies at Scott. Again the Kumbis wrote the Colemans:

> We do feel your fellowship while I am writing this letter to you. How nice it will be to be in a circle and have fellowship as two families. We with you will have *injera* and *doro wut* for lunch! ...Nathanael is now big enough that he starts to wear Nathan's clothes sent to him. He is a very happy boy.... We are praying for you and your church. His mighty power moves in weak servants like you and I. How wonderful it is to serve the Lord. I Cor. 15:58.

At Christmas time, Negussie said he was sending "the final Christmas greetings from Scott Theological College. Next year it will be directly from Ethiopia, or you might come to spend the holidays with us!"

During Negussie's last term, Fantaye's time drew near to deliver a second child. Again, Meseret came to help Fantaye when she delivered, while Negussie cared for Nathanael and kept up his studies at home. Negussie was struggling to finish his course work and papers. Often he suffered from asthma, though he didn't complain.

The new child, also a son, they named Nebeyu, which meant "his prophet." Meseret stayed nights at the hospital for a week, nursing the mother and child. Later she visited them back in Machakos. Negussie seemed so much more engaged in the life of the children than most Ethiopian fathers. He helped discipline his child, warning him when he misbehaved, and giving him spanks when needed.

At Easter time, Canadian missionaries Jean and Soula Isch were passing through Nairobi. Negussie's saga had challenged them and they had prayed for him for years. They contacted Negussie and arranged a rendezvous. It was a wonderful time, meeting him and his family. However, they noticed Negussie was coughing a lot and did not seem to feel really well.

As the time to return to Ethiopia drew near, Fantaye found herself wishing they could stay on in Kenya. They weighed the suggestion that they remain abroad to take further studies. Many a bright seminarian had done that, but Negussie did not want to do so. It was rebuilding time in Ethiopia, and he was eager to do his part. Still, he wondered if he should help his wife obtain some skills while out of the country — like learning to type and use a computer so she could help him in the ministry.

The final term was a difficult one. Little Nebie required an infant's care right when Negussie was pushing hard to finish his course. His desire to begin serving in Ethiopia was passionate and he longed to receive fuller power for service. "I'm planning to take my first month there," he told Fantaye, "just to go before the Lord."

A few weeks before graduation, he began struggling more with kidney and breathing problems. Alarmed, Meseret out at Kijabe arranged with the mission to have a car go and take him to Kijabe Hospital. The diagnosis was typhoid. Struggling to carry through, he got up too soon. Negussie's legs became more and more swollen, and even walking became difficult. His friends observed how very ill he was and, with Fantaye, felt they must not let him leave, but must get him well in Kenya, where better health care was available.

But their scholarship money ran out. Alternatives narrowed down. And so it was that Fantaye packed up their few things. Friends took the little family to the Nairobi airport. At takeoff, Fantaye wept with a deep sense of foreboding. When they arrived in Ethiopia, her husband went straight to a hospital. Negussie was sick, sicker than anyone knew.

THE BEGINNING

The hour of embarkation upon Negussie's long-cherished dream swiftly turned into a nightmare. He spent a little time at his brother's home in Addis, but the days became a blur of transfers between clinics and hospitals.

When his old friend heard of Negussie's illness, he rushed to him. "It was heartbreaking to me," Mulugeta remembers, "that after his graduation this should happen. I could tell he was really sick, but we talked; he even teased a little. He told me he had a breathing problem, that he was very tired, had lost his appetite, and was under treatment. They took him to the Universal Clinic, where he was an in-patient for a week. His body was swelling. 'Well, if I die, I have no fear at all,' he said. 'Just pray for me. If I die, I'll go to face my Lord.' But he loved his wife deeply. When he thought of her, it brought tears."

Negussie and John had been corresponding as each finished studies and looked to the future. By now, John and Phyllis were actively pursuing the possibility of coming to Ethiopia, and the senior Colemans were already there. Actually it was John's younger brother, Dan, who got there before John did. Dan had long wished to introduce his wife to his childhood home. John prepared a letter for Dan to carry personally to Negussie. In it John stated their situation:

Please excuse us for not writing to you for such a long time. At first I was delaying because I was waiting to hear the news of whether we were accepted by SIM to come to Ethiopia. It took five months for that to become completely finalized. Also, I have been very busy with the two little churches here and with my studies. I am sorry that I allowed these things to keep me from writing to you.

So we are anxious to hear your news. I am sure you also have been through a very busy time and a time of transition... Please keep on praying for us! It seems that we are coming to important crossroads in our lives. We have applied to go with SIM to Ethiopia for a year and we have been accepted, but some important things have to be done in order for us to be able to come. We are confident that God will provide us with a team of prayer and financial partners for this ministry. I also know that God has a preparation work to do in our hearts so that we are serving Him in the right spirit and attitude...I am so happy for Dan that he can take his wife to visit his childhood homeland. Also to be honest, I am very jealous of him! But in time we will have our chance to come too, I believe....

When Dan and Wendy arrived in July of l993, Murray and Bea Coleman were working in Hosanna, a long drive from Addis. Dan had not been as close to Negussie as John was, but he had looked up to him as a big brother, too. Negussie had sent notes to "Danny" sometimes, with his letters to John. While still in the capital after Dan and Wendy's plane came in, the senior and junior Colemans discovered Negussie was ill and they all went to find him. His condition shocked them. He lay on an examining table awaiting admission to the National Polyclinic and had been given injections. They left full of concern, but had to go back down country.

"Why have the sufferings of Job come upon me?" he asked once in his pain. With medication he got relief, but Fantaye was horrified when she saw how bloated his body had become. Trying to protect her from concern, he told her good night in the normal way, but after she left he whispered to a nurse, "I won't last the night."

For people who questioned him later, Mulugeta had to summarize the quick progression of Negussie's illness: "The doctor advised his brother to take him to the Black Lion Hospital to get oxygen assistance. He took him. But before they were able to give the oxygen, Negussie went to be with the Lord. *Kidney failure after earlier typhoid complications,* they wrote down as the cause of death. Negussie was only forty-one. We were all in shock. We took his body to his brother's home, and people started coming from Addis and Wolisso. The service was at the Meserete Heywet Church. We buried his body at St. Joseph's cemetery on Debre Zeit road. No one was prepared for his death."

Pastor Kaydamo wept and told a close friend, "I wish I could have died instead of Negussie. I should have died and he lived."

Ato Tekle, who had followed so many prisoners' sagas, sat in mourning along with his son-in-law, Mulugeta. Negussie's mourners ranged from family to friends, from Wolisso to Asmara, from Kenya to America, from pastors to prisoners, from students to teachers, from old to young.

Crowds came to the Meserete Heywet church for the funeral, during which Ato Kaydamo spoke. With the Apostle Paul they affirmed that believers need not "grieve like the rest of men, who have no hope." From the word of God, they took comfort in glimpses of the magnificent life into which Christians enter when they step into His presence. The Savior explained his own death in terms of a principle that would work out in His people's lives: "Except a corn of wheat fall into the ground and die, it abideth alone: but if it die, it bringeth forth much fruit."

Like many others, Sahle was cut to the heart when he found out. Someone had told him Negussie was asking to see him, but he'd not yet gone to his side. To nearly everyone who knew their story, this ending seemed incredible.

It was inscrutable to Fantaye most of all. She had waited all those years. Now in her mid-thirties, overnight she had become a widow with two little sons, one two and a half, the other five months old. She was stunned. Nathanael cried continually for his daddy. She nursed Nebie, hardly able to bear the grief.

Thursday morning's mission radio dispatch shocked the Colemans to attention as the announcement came over the crackling airwaves that Negussie had died on Wednesday morning. Going to town to make a phone call to Addis, they learned that the service was taking place that very hour. There was no way they could cover the distance from Hosanna that fast, but a whole busload of Wolisso people did get to the funeral.

Over in Canada, John Coleman put down the phone after his parents' call, devastated.

On Friday, July 16th, Bea sat down at a typewriter in Hosanna, heavy hearted, and wrote a long letter to John and Sharon's families in Canada:

> We drove in to town last night to phone you John to let you know about Negussie's death and we presume that all of you have heard by now. We would like to give some detail as we have heard it. Our minds just could not take in that he was with the Lord when we heard it on the radio yesterday morning. He graduated in April and then became sick... On July 7th they brought him to the Mission and our doctor examined him but said unless there was a battery of tests, he could not tell just by symptomatic diagnosis. They tried to get him into the Black Lion Hospital but there was not space so he was taken to a Poly Clinic where he was given tests.... We saw him in the afternoon after Dan

and Wendy got to Addis on the 9th. He was very un-
comfortable and could only speak in a little over a whisper but he knew us all and welcomed Dan and Wendy
very warmly in his usual way. He said to Dan, "Wel-
come home!" We did not talk long because he obvi-
ously was in real discomfort. He was very bloated looking... Dan and Wendy had brought some clothing gifts
for their little boys so they were able to give them to
Fantaye whom we met outside. We also gave her your
letter John, and Dad was able to hand her some money.
We do not know if Negussie ever read your letter but
we trust so... Sunday we went again to visit Negussie
in the afternoon. He was much brighter, much of the
bloatedness seemed to have subsided and he said he
was sleeping well. He was smiling — his voice was
strong and we visited briefly with him.... Somehow our
hearts were at peace that he was over the worst.

We do not know what transpired but got the message on the radio yesterday that he passed away about
noon on Wednesday, the 14th, and was buried about
noon yesterday from the Meserete Heywet (Geja)
church. We heard on the radio this morning that it was
a very sad funeral and Ato Kaydamo counseled people
not to blame God but to accept as His will what He had
done.

While waiting for more explanation after the phone call,
before his parents' letter came in the post, John pondered the
loss of his best friend. Never had the passage in II Samuel
recording David's lamentation over Jonathan's death been more
real to him. He could have rent his own clothes over his fallen
brother, a man who'd been "anointed" in John's eyes. He poured
out his grief on paper:

Negussie, how can I say what you meant to us? You

were like a big brother to us when we were kids. I could say that you were the first and best friend I ever had, but you were more than that. You were family. You embraced us and we embraced you. A thousand memories flood my mind as I think of the years we had together. You were so gentle and patient with us when we were little. You were like a guide to us in more than one way — not just showing us the path to the spring or the bridge (the "spridge," we called it, when we were being crazy) and teaching us the best games like stone tag, but you were a role model and mentor to us. You were just enough older to be our leader but young enough or humble enough, was it, to be a peer too. We learned so many things from you. Graciousness, contentment, simplicity, thankfulness... is there a word for the attitude you took toward life? You were certainly full of joy and so much fun to be with!

You didn't talk to us that much about yourself, your own family, life at school, and such. Maybe you talked with Mom and Dad more about those things. I remember Mom saying that whenever you were asked about your back and having TB of the spine, you would respond by thanking God that because of that illness you heard the good news about Christ...

I remember some of the talks we used to have together when I would walk to the big zigaba tree with you when it was time for you to go home. You had wonderful dreams about the future, of getting an education and doing something for your country. Every time our family had to come home to Canada, we would pledge our friendship to each other. I will never forget the last time that I saw you in the summer of '75. We were living at the Press and I walked to the gate with you and said good-bye, I think both in Ethiopian fashion and with a big hug. Little did I know that I would have to wait until heaven to see you again.

But you wrote me so many letters. I'm glad I saved most of them. They are full of praises to God despite difficulties that you faced, full of encouragements to me to love the Lord with all my heart. I have letters from you from Obi, from Asmara, from... and all of them radiate with that same sincere love for the Lord and His people. You guys, you and Tesfaye and the others really stuck together and urged one another on to love the Lord and live for him. Your dedication and sincere love just radiated from your lives. What a privilege it is to have known you and been your friend!

As John read and reread Negussie's letters that spanned eighteen years, he saw them in a new light now that he was a pastor shepherding a flock. *Why, Negussie was teaching me how to be a disciple all those years,* he realized. The letters said little about Negussie's personal trials, but much about Christ's sufficiency to meet every need. He would recommend to John some scripture that had encouraged him. *I was always his junior,* John mused. *He lit my candle. He was always light-years ahead of me.*

When they were able to return to Addis shortly after the funeral, the senior Colemans went to see Fantaye and the family. They spoke of their great love for Negussie, and especially of John's.

Their letter written two day's after Negussie's death finally reached John and he wrote back quickly:

I just couldn't deal with this very well until I knew more detail. I was really feeling bad that I haven't written him much over this past year. I guess the nagging question in my mind was, if we'd known he was sick maybe there would have been something we could have done to aid his recovery. But I was comforted by your letter. I'm so glad that you sent him a graduation card and letter and the Lord worked out the timing that you passed along our money for Fantaye at that time. It was just when they would have needed it.... I'm sure that the family and friends at the funeral and in Wolisso found themselves asking why. Why would God take him now after years of what looked like to us to be His preparation of a very special servant? I guess God's values and His ways are not ours....

This death stirred deep thought. In some ways, death by disease is harder to fathom than heroic martyrdom is. People tried to deal with Negussie's untimely death, trying to absorb its meaning. In some ways, sudden martyrdom was not more costly than the grueling daily price people like Negussie chose to pay.

Derege, an editor who published a Christian magazine underground during Derg times, interviewed many and put together a powerful summary of Negussie's life testimony. Thousands read the magazine. In the article, Negussie's half-sister Alemaz shared memories from their childhood, saying as she pondered his life, "He seemed to be a man created for suffering — and yet, he was always smiling." She perceived that her brother was a man of God quite early in his life. "The secret things of God were revealed to him. He was a thankful person, a loving person, a humble person. Until the end, he was a man of praise."

Fantaye was still struggling to trust God in this loss. In the interview with Derege, she tried to relate a few significant segments of their life story for the article. This was being a tremendous test of her own faith. She could hardly speak of Negussie without tearing up. Little things would undo her. Someone asked for his guitar, but it was to her a symbol of his suffering, and she could not give it up. She was honest about her deep grief, with which many who had suffered could identify. Someone had pointed her to a passage from Isaiah 57 which specially helped her, she said: "The righteous perish, and no one ponders it in his heart; devout men are taken away, and no one understands that the righteous are taken away to be spared from evil. Those who walk uprightly enter into peace; they find rest as they lie in death." The published testimony of Negussie's life strengthened and challenged many that did not even know him.

Like many that loved Negussie, Mulugeta kept mulling over the tragedy. He finally settled it in his mind. "God has his own plan. Negussie had contributed his life for the gospel of Jesus Christ in a communist state. He'd been naked, beaten, tortured. He'd shouldered that great responsibility with the Lord's assistance. We used to think, *If Negussie is able to shoulder this, although weak, what about those of us who are stronger?* Even after his graduation, what more did the Lord want? He had completed his task. The Lord gave him rest."

When Negussie's relative living abroad got word of this death, boyhood memories came flooding back — Negussie rarely without a smile, his gracious spirit, his joy, even when subjected to so much pain. This deeply spiritual man was profoundly troubled over Negussie's being taken so young and kept asking himself what God was doing.

"Except for the question that led me to the Lord, the question of Negussie's death was the hardest of my life," he said later. "I kept mulling over the early apostles' experience in Acts. Some died early. While one was killed, another was let out of prison. *That's my right,* the Lord seemed to be saying to me, *It was not that James or Peter was better. That's my choice, my purpose.*"

This brilliant Ethiopian had become an unusually fruitful man in God' service and was strongly dedicated to spiritual productivity. He kept pondering the meaning of Negussie's life and death. Finally a profound understanding came to him, one which was to change his life: "All this caused me to face a realistic assessment of what ministry is about," he told John Coleman later. In that moment of insight, he felt God was revealing to him a truth: *Ministry is not an activity, it is total obedience to my revealed will for your life as long as you live; it is not what you produce. Negussie finished his service. He was not to teach and preach, he was just to obey, without title, without pay. He accomplished his ministry.*

Faithful to the Lamb of God, Negussie chose the path of the cross to glory.   A seed has been planted and has not "remained alone."   There are thousands who have stepped into a new beginning of faith and obedience because of the challenge of this man's life. God be praised!

EPILOGUE

People puzzled by Negussie's departure went back to the Lord's words and pondered their contemporary outworking. In every generation, death makes us take inventory of life. Languishing in grief when Jesus was buried, the disciples searched back and found this word that He had given them on the eve of the crucifixion: "Truly, truly I say to you, unless a grain of wheat falls into the earth and dies, it remains alone; but if it dies, it bears much fruit." Christ's death had gathered up all in Adam, and His resurrection had brought sons and daughters into the Father's kingdom, a millionfold.

How had Negussie's particular life fulfilled the Messiah's promise? When Christ's torchbearers cross the finish line into Glory, they pass their baton. Negussie's passed into the hands of a relay of compatriots the extent of which only God could know. Some stood forth quickly. Within a year, John Coleman was enabled to gather up his family and began to work in Ethiopia. Negussie's relative pressed on for the cause of Christ in the world, training Third World leadership in twenty-some nations. At night he and his wife labored on studies in Amharic designed to strengthen the church in Ethiopia. Sahle became head of a Christian publishing company. Here and there, an Ethiopian who knew Negussie calls his example to mind when a test or challenge comes. Prisoners remember their cellmate's shepherding, and friends his counseling. When a funeral procession passes by on a street, Negussie's sudden passing speaks again, *Do it now, while you yet have time.*

For Fantaye, the race is requiring another lap of separation before that great Day of reunion, that Wedding Feast their marriage had foreshadowed. Not spared from widowhood, she shares the lot of a host of Ethiopian and Eritrean women who lost their husbands in these difficult years. As Negussie's lot was shared with unbelievers suffering in prison, Fantaye's now is mingled with unbelievers who are suffering outside. Thus the world is exposed to the difference God can make in a life. Fantaye's brothers soon saw the difference, trusted Him, and began to reach out to others themselves.

Having returned to her parents' home again, she prays for strength for the godly nurturing of Negussie's sons. In the little time she's been able to salvage, she has sought out classes to acquire skills Negussie had wanted her to get. She has had to depend heavily upon her heavenly Bridegroom. When the youngest son was three, she changed his name. "Because of what I've been through," she said, "I've changed Nebie's name to *Mikias.*" Mikias means "there is no one like God."

Negussie's story so touched on the elemental challenges of life, that it spread abroad, as have the sagas of God's people over the ages. Never strong or famous or rich or privileged, a humble man had simply been faithful. Few Christians have less natural endowments. His life story spoke the needed word. Chris told it to Germans, the Hsuehs to Asians, the Isches to French-speaking Africans, and many shared it in the English-speaking world. Each generation has those who join the ranks of those whose lives speak to us. "Abel," Hebrews 11 says of a young man, "although dead, yet speaketh."

Negussie was representative of many Ethiopian believers whose lives and deaths exalted their Lord. His saga serves as a metaphor for the body of Christ: crippled, suffering, of mixed blood, poor, captured, freed, but "always carrying in the body the death of Jesus, so that the life of Jesus may also be manifested in our bodies." Still, just as Negussie was rich, Ethiopia's believers are a community rich in God. Like his, theirs is a royal destiny.

They now face onslaughts from the age-old Enemy in new forms. His use of Marxist strategy may have failed, but smoldering ethnic rivalries can serve as deadly flames to fan. Already the peace is broken, and famine keeps raising its head.

The Body of Christ in Ethiopia is a deeply eschatological community. These brothers and sisters born from our Father bear a unique message to the wider body. "Hear what I am saying to the churches," our Lord has told us. "Watch!" What will be the next move of the Spirit of God among them, a move in which the whole Body has a stake?

GLOSSARY

(Amharic to English)

alem	world
Ato	Mr.
Beta Israel	House of Israel (also known as Falashas or Black Jews)
cadre	young person assigned by the Party to promote Marxism
Derg	"Committee of Equals" (ruling body during Ethiopian Revolution)
Ethiopia Tikdem	"Ethiopia First" - Ethiopian Revolution slogan
Falasha	"landless" or "foreigner" (term for the Black Jews, also called Beta Israel)
ferenge	foreigner
gabi	heavy cotton shawl
Ge'ez	holy language of Coptic and Ethiopian Orthodox worship

Haile Selassie	"power of the Trinity" (the Emperor's title)
injera and *wut*	the Ethiopian national food (flat pancake-like bread and hotly spiced stew)
inset	false banana plant
Kale Heywet (KHC)	"Word of Life" (SIM background church)
kebele	a neighborhood political association, a rural or urban commune
Kibra Nagast	"the Glory of Kings" document
Mekane Yesus (EECMY)	"Place where Jesus Dwells" (Lutheran back ground church)
Meserete Kristos (MKC)	"Christ the Foundation" (Mennonite background church)
Meserete Heywet	"Foundation of Life" (one of the KHC churches in Addis Ababa)
meskel	cross
Meskel	holiday celebrating "the finding of the true cross"
mesob	basket-woven circular low table used for serving *injera* and *wut*
negus	King
Negussie	my king
Negus Nagast	King of Kings
Pente	short for "Pentecostal": actually, designation for any non-Orthodox, non-Catholic Christian in Ethiopia

ras	head, or duke
Tabot	Ark of the Covenant
teff	a cereal indigenous to Ethiopia, the flour used in making *injera* (flat bread)
Timkat	Orthodox holiday in January commemorating Christ's baptism
wut	name for highly spiced stews (meat and vegetable) which are dipped into with *injera* bread
Yehadig	coalition of fronts that drove out the *Derg* in 1991
Yesus	Jesus
zemecha	Amharic for "campaign," i.e. Development Through Cooperation Campaign, required of students